Tinsel, Tumbleweeds and Star-Spangled Celebrations

Tinsel, Tumbleweeds, and Star-Spangled Celebrations

Holidays on the Western Frontier from New Year's to Christmas

★ SHERRY MONAHAN ★

TWODOT®

GUILFORD, CONNECTICUT
HELENA, MONTANA

A · TWODOT® · BOOK

An imprint of Globe Pequot
A registered trademark of Rowman & Littlefield

Distributed by NATIONAL BOOK NETWORK

British Library Cataloguing in Publication Information available
Library of Congress Cataloging-in-Publication Data available

ISBN 978-1-4930-1802-4 (paperback)
ISBN 978-1-4930-1803-1 (e-book)

 The paper used in this publication meets the minimum requirements of American National Standard for Information Sciences—Permanence of Paper for Printed Library Materials, ANSI/NISO Z39.48-1992.

Printed in the United States of America

CONTENTS

WILD WEST CELEBRATIONS

"WE'D HAD A RIGHT GOOD CHRISTMAS DINNER. WE STILL HAD some nuts left over and some of the peppermint candy Virge liked," wrote Virgil Earp's wife Allie. She recalled that fond memory while living in Tombstone, Arizona, in the early 1880s. It's hard to imagine Virgil Earp, Annie Oakley, or Jesse James sitting down to a plate of peppermint candy during the Christmas season. It's not exactly the image we conjure when we think of the Wild West or the rough-and-tumble days of the frontier, but it's true. Virgil Earp and his famous brothers, Calamity Jane, Wild Bill Hickok, and miners, cowboys, dance hall girls, businessmen, and regular citizens celebrated our national holidays on the frontier. From the mid-nineteenth to the early twentieth century, as pioneers, adventurers, settlers, and fortune seekers settled the West from Kansas to California, people forging their new lives still enjoyed sending a sweet or funny cupid on Valentine's Day, coloring Easter eggs, having picnics and eating ice cream on July Fourth, eating turkey and playing football on Thanksgiving, decorating and wrapping gifts for Christmas, and having elegant parties on New Year's.

Even though the West was still not fully settled and many lived in remote locations, the Victorian trends of the East prevailed in cities. And even in smaller settlements and tiny homesteads, holidays could be celebrated and decorated with the latest Victorian trends—even if they were accomplished on a small-scale or with homemade versions.

Decorations, food, and gifts may have been modified by pioneers based on the trends back East, but distance and resources did not stop them from celebrating or keeping up family traditions. Pioneer women embraced their surroundings and adapted to them. They wanted their holidays to mimic what they had back home.

This book looks at the traditions and fun ways the pioneers celebrated all the popular holidays that we still celebrate today. Included are some firsthand accounts, some recipes, decorating tips, gift ideas, and more. Please note that all the recipes are from historic Western newspapers or cookbooks. However, it wasn't always possible to find a recipe from, for example, a Nebraska, Wyoming, or Colorado newspaper or cookbook to match a Nebraska, Wyoming, or Colorado story, so then one from another state was used instead.

HAPPY PIONEER HOLIDAYS!

CHAPTER ONE

NEW YEAR'S

———————— ⦚ ————————

GENERAL GEORGE ARMSTRONG CUSTER AND HIS WIFE, ELIZABETH Bacon Custer, donned their finest and sat in their parlor in Leavenworth, Kansas, waiting for callers on January 1, 1868. Rebecca Richmond, Mrs. Custer's favorite cousin, was with them, and she wrote, "General Custer and his wife, Anna Darrah, Charles Kendall, Mary and I were stationed in the front parlor at one o'clock today to receive the callers and pass others along to the refreshment table in the back room. We were honored by about forty calls. . . . Messrs Weir, Bell, Hale, Jackson and Cooke spent the evening with us and we had some music. Major Bell brought 'Silence!' a very pretty serenade, and he with some of the other gentlemen sang it beautifully."

The ringing out of the old year and the ringing in of the new was a time for celebration on the frontier, just as it is today. New Year's Eve might be celebrated with balls and parties; New Year's Day offered a special chance for friends and neighbors to informally call on each other and offer gifts and cards. And so from the plains of Kansas to the big cities across the West, pioneers visited one another's homes to celebrate on New Year's Day.

Gentlemen, both married and single, were generally the callers, while ladies opened their homes to friends, families, and neighbors dressed in their holiday best. The gents wore their finest trousers, white shirts, colored vests, and formal jackets. The ladies curled their up-dos, wrapped themselves tightly in corsets, and layered their "unmentionables" under their silk and brocaded dresses. Gifts were often exchanged on New Year's Eve and Day, but the gifts given to start the New Year were often practical rather than whimsical. Most visits included some form of music, and many people danced. Tables were laden with holiday delicacies and treats as well. Pioneers enjoyed each other's company and sometimes outdoor activities where the weather permitted.

In 1886 a Dallas newspaper reported that everyone across the West was following "The Time-Honored Custom of Making Calls Extensively Observed and Elegant Evening Receptions Held Throughout the City." Bonbon making and taffy-pull parties were popular to entertain the "young folks," while dancing, singing, games, and music were enjoyed by the adults. Balls and parties were also popular across the

A funny calling card was used by some men in Topeka, Kansas, for making New Year's Day visits in 1901. TOPEKA DAILY CAPITAL, JANUARY 2, 1901

frontier and were held by fraternal organizations, social clubs, businesses, and private residents.

Watch Parties

In many places a New Year's Eve party was called a "Watch Party" as revelers watched Father Time deliver the New Year.

The *Denver Post* reported on their city's watch parties:

> *Society is going to take a much-needed rest next week. Everyone is worn out with the Christmas festivities, and everyone has eaten and drunk so much that all are on the verge of dyspepsia. It has been an unusually gay holiday season. . . . During the week there were New Year's watch parties, New Year's receptions, several children's dances, dinners, card parties, and [a] number of more formal dinners and luncheons for the "grown ups," but nothing in the*

This much-welcomed postcard was sent and received by many a pioneer (ca. 1900s). SHERRY MONAHAN

Colorful New Year's postcard with birds (ca. 1900s). SHERRY MONAHAN

nature of real function except the El Paso club at Colorado Springs. The watch parties were mostly jolly, informal affairs, at which people gathered around them their intimate friends to watch the new century in. The El Paso club ball was, of course, an elaborate, swell and exclusive affair.

Public Celebrations

Singing was heard in the Congregational Church during the first week of January 1875 in Santa Barbara, California. The church's Sunday school had a holiday theme, and they decorated an olive tree with local oranges to ring in the New Year. While some people

Men and woman enjoy a New Year's picnic at Mission Creek, California in 1875. COURTESY OF
THE NEW YORK PUBLIC LIBRARY

attended church, others enjoyed a picnic at nearby Mission Creek. Several men and
women packed picnic baskets and headed to the creek. They laid a large cloth on the
ground and enjoyed wine and likely leftovers from the holidays.

Nebraskan Ella Oblinger penned a New Year's letter to her grandparents:

January 4, 1883. I take my pen in hand with much pleasure tonight to scratch you a few words. . . . New-Years I got a circle-comb, and some candy. New-Years Day I went to St. Peter . . . went to see the Asylum but we couldn't get in; their help [staff] was all gone but two or three persons but on we drove around the building [that] is somewhere between 15 or 20 rods long. Then we all went to the photograph gallery and they all had their pictures taken.

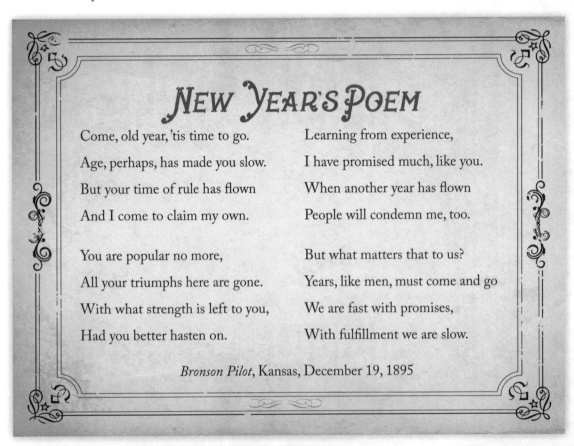

New Year's Poem

Come, old year, 'tis time to go.
Age, perhaps, has made you slow.
But your time of rule has flown
And I come to claim my own.

You are popular no more,
All your triumphs here are gone.
With what strength is left to you,
Had you better hasten on.

Learning from experience,
I have promised much, like you.
When another year has flown
People will condemn me, too.

But what matters that to us?
Years, like men, must come and go
We are fast with promises,
With fulfillment we are slow.

Bronson Pilot, Kansas, December 19, 1895

Dining Out in Style

San Francisco was a bustling city by 1892, and its residents celebrated New Year's Day in style. Dining out at the luxurious Palace Hotel was a special treat that not everyone could afford. But those who could were pampered. The extensive menu included over one hundred wines, liquors, liqueurs, and more. Dinner began with clams and oysters, followed by green turtle, consommé, and puree of goose soups. Hors d'oeuvres included radishes, olives, and celery. The fish course included trout and fillet of sole served with duchess potatoes. Following that was a course of Virginia ham with Champagne sauce. For the main entrees, diners could choose from spring chicken, filet mignon, lamb steak, and mallard duck. Assorted vegetables included asparagus on toast, artichokes with hollandaise sauce, mashed potatoes, squash, boiled rice, French peas, French string beans, and baked sweet potatoes. Roman punch was served next to cleanse the palate before the next course of cold meats, which included beef, chicken, turkey, goose, lamb, veal, and mutton. As if that wasn't enough already, patrons needed to loosen their waistbands, because the roast course was next. It included prime ribs of beef, teal duck, mallard duck, lamb, goose, stuffed turkey, fresh pork, veal, and domestic duck. The salad course followed this and included lobster, *doucette*, and romaine. Anyone who had room for dessert could choose from English plum pudding with rum or hard sauce; apricot and pear tartlets; mince, apple, and pumpkin pies; and coconut cream sandwiches. The meal ended with ices that included orange water, and strawberry and pistachio ice creams.

EGGNOG

Eggnog was a popular holiday beverage in the 1880s, and 1,200 eggs were used just in Tombstone, Arizona, alone to make the New Year's Day eggnog in 1889. It was also in 1889 when a new fashionable trend was reported by Denver's *Weekly News*. While eggnog itself was grand, serving it in a traditional glass was blasé; the new glass trend was a hollowed-out orange. To make it, a small top was cut off, and the orange cleaned out. The eggnog was poured in and the top was placed back on the orange. Two straws were tied with a ribbon and used to sip the creamy libation.

The Rose Parade

The first annual rose parade was held in Pasadena, California, on New Year's Day in 1890. Harris Newmark was the son of a modest Prussian Jewish merchant who sailed to America in 1853 to join his older brother in Los Angeles. He made a fortune in real estate, the wholesale grocery business, and hides and wools, becoming a leader in the local Jewish community and the city at large. He recalled the first Tournament of Roses parade, "There were . . . sports, but the principal event was a parade of vehicles of every description which, moving along under the graceful burden of their beautiful floral decorations, presented a magnificent and typically Southern California winter sight. The tournament was so successful that it has become an annual event participated in by many and attracting visitors from near and far."

According to the Tournament of Roses history timeline, members of the Valley Hunt Club voted to hold a parade of flower-decorated horses and buggies and an afternoon of public games on the "town lot" east of Los Robles between Colorado and Santa Fe on January 1, 1890. They wanted the parade to be an American version of the festival of roses in Nice, France. After the parade ended, young men competed in a variety of foot races, tugs of war, jousts and a tourney of rings—an old Spanish game in which mounted horsemen, each carrying a 12-foot lance, try to spear three rings hung about 30 feet apart while riding at top speed. Because of the floral displays, professor Charles F. Holder, who was the event's first president, declared, "Now we have the name we want—'The Tournament of Roses.'" More than 2,000 people attended the first Tournament. Because the parade had become too big for the Valley Hunt Club to manage, the Tournament of Roses Association was formed. Other year's event included races of all kinds including, ranchman's, steeple chase, flat, dressing, bicycle, pony trotting, egg and spoon, and donkey.

Photograph of a horse-drawn carriage decorated with Marcheneil roses and labeled "Happy New Year" at 313 South Spring Street during the Tournament of the Roses Parade, Pasadena, California, 1906. Several fancy-dressed ladies with parasols and a driver are aboard. Fleurs-de-lis are visible on several banners. COURTESY OF THE UNIVERSITY OF SOUTHERN CALIFORNIA LIBRARY AND THE CALIFORNIA HISTORICAL SOCIETY

Nine men sit in an open automobile that is decorated with flowers at the Pasadena Tournament of Roses celebration (1903). Most of the men are wearing ribbons on the breasts of their jackets and hats with ribbons. Two children are sitting on the curb behind the car. Two horses are visible at left. Trees and a few houses are visible in the background. COURTESY OF THE UNIVERSITY OF SOUTHERN CALIFORNIA LIBRARY AND THE CALIFORNIA HISTORICAL SOCIETY

Five years later the first Rose Bowl game was played at Tournament Park and Stanford University played the University of Michigan. Stanford was routed 49–0. The expected crowd was to be about 1,000, but over 8,500 spectators came to the game. While the crowd stampeded after the game like frightened cattle, no one was injured, but it would be another fourteen years before a Rose Bowl game would be played.

Mina Dean Halsey was a New York writer who visited California and wrote about the Rose parade:

> *New Year's Day I went over to Pasadena to the Tournament of Roses. This is a "doings" held in the Crown City every year, and the natives and tourists for miles around come to admire the show. Just why it is called the Tournament of Roses, I don't know. To be sure, there are some roses, more carnations, and mostly geraniums. But right here let me say that the geraniums in California, are the finest flowers you ever set eyes on. By gum, they are prettier than half the roses back home, for the bunches of blossoms on each stalk are as big as my two fists, and the color of 'em is away beyond anything I can describe to you. A hedge of these scarlet beauties beat a hedge of bum roses anytime and anywhere, even back home in Illinois. Them's my sentiments, only don't let the editor of the home paper get hold of it, Bill. I owe him a little money and I don't want to get him riled up. The floats were all right, and some pretty girls, a few, were mixed in among the flowers, but Los Angeles flowers and Los Angeles girls knock 'em all to holler.*

Festivities and Feasts

In stark contrast to California's sunny, warm weather, Kansas City, Missouri, celebrated the arrival of 1891 in high style with parties, theater events, and a wicked snowstorm. One local paper reported, "The snow commenced[,] . . . a blustering wind arose, and the thermometer dropped a few notches below freezing." Despite the weather, the manager of the Western Sash and Door Company threw a banquet for associates and employees. The menu included oysters in cream, ham with champagne sauce, lobster salad, Saratoga chips, champagne punch, rum-based Roman punch in between courses as a palate cleanser, angel food cake, lady fingers, bananas, oranges, and nuts.

Any Victorian knew that Roman punch could cause someone to be a little tipsy, but ginger ale was tricky. It was sold as both a nonalcoholic soda and a fermented product. It would seem that imbiber Mr. E. S. Park of Denver, Colorado, had enjoyed too much of the fermented version. The paper described him as an "enthusiastic young man," who decided to shoot out the stars in front of city hall on New Year's Eve in 1893. He rang in the New Year in jail, where he was reportedly locked up for safekeeping.

The following year, Tacoma, Washington's *Daily News* expressed a sentiment that was a little too late for men like the ginger-ale-loving Mr. Park. In their New Year's Day paper, they wrote, "This is the day you swear off, that is if you are a man and have been given even in the very slightest degree to touching of the liquids that make the mind dizzy with pleasure and the head throb with pain subsequently as a gentle reminder of the joys that you have been flirting with."

Hotels across the frontier offered New Year's Eve and Day meals for those who could or wanted to skip a meal at home. In Tacoma, Washington, on January 1, 1894, the Hotel Chilberg's restaurant served a very elaborate New Year's Day meal with over seventy items on the menu. The menu, equally elaborate, was three pages long with each item being priced a la carte. In addition to the meal, they offered a free mandolin concert by the Apollo Mandolin Club from Illinois to entertain patrons. The hotel's chef took advantage of the abundance of local fish and game to enhance his menu. He included speckled trout, Columbia River salmon, Chinook salmon, duck, grouse, and venison.

Another Pacific Northwest restaurant, the Portland, in Oregon had an elaborate New Year's Day dinner in 1895 that included local dishes. Their colorful menu offered diners striped bass and quail. They also offered oysters, turkey, and beef dishes.

OUR NEW YEAR DINNER.
JANUARY 1, 1894.

OYSTERS.

Olympias, on Plate.............................. 25
Eastern, on Half Shell......................... 25

SOUP.

Green Turtle, a l' Anglaise.................... 10
Chicken Gumbo, á la Creole.................. 10
Consommé, Celestine........................... 05

FISH.

Broiled Speckled Trout, Maitre d' Hotel......... 35
Baked Columbia River Smelts, a l' Espagnole.... 25   Side 10
Boiled Chinook Salmon, Anchovie Sauce 25   Side 10

BOILED.

Young Turkey, Celery Sauce................... 50
Smoked Ox Tongue, With Greens............. 25
Boiled Sugar Cured Ham, Sherry Wine Sauce..... 25

ENTREES.

Bottle of Claret or White Wine Served with 50c Dinner.

Vol au Vent of Oysters, á la Bechamel......... 40
Croquettes of Fresh Crabs Deviled............ 40
Chicken Sauté, a la Maringo.................. 50
Breast of Pheasant Larded, with French Peas...... 50
Broiled Butter Ball Duck with Water Cress....... 50
Small Tenderloin Steak, á la Bernaise......... 40
Brochette of Turkey Livers on Toast with Mushrooms.. 40
Venison Chops Sauté, Sauce Poivrade......... 35
Calves Head en Tortue........................ 35
Breast of Veal Fricassee with Oysters........ 25
Baked Lamb Pie with Dumplings, Country Style.... 25
Spanish Puffs Glace, au Cognac............... 10

Old Port Punch............................. 10

GAME.

Baked Mallard Duck, Stuffed, Celery Dressing...... 50
Roast Blue Grouse, Oyster Dressing.......... 50
Saddle of Venison with Jelly................ 35

POULTRY.

Roast Young Turkey Stuffed, Cranberry Sauce...... 50
Green Goose Stuffed with Baked Apples........ 50
Roast Young Chicken, Giblet Sauce.......... 50

ROASTS.

Loin of Pork, Apple Sauce................... 30
Ribs of Prime Beef, Dish Gravy............. 25
Saddle of Mutton with Jelly................ 25
Shoulder of Veal with Dressing............. 25

VEGETABLES.

Mashed Potatoes.   Boiled Potatoes.   Succotash,
Cauliflower, 10.   String Beans, 10c.   Boiled Rice, 10c.
Sugar Corn, á la Creme, 10c.
Green Peas, 10c.   Stewed Tomatoes, 5c.   French Peas, 25c.
Sweet Potatoes Baked, Extra, 10c.

COLD DISHES AND SALADS.

Chicken Salad, Mayonaise..................... 15
Fresh Crab Salad............................ 15
Chicken.................................... 40
Ham.. 25
Tongue..................................... 25

RELISHES.

Queen Olives, 10c.   Celery, 15c.   Chutney, 10c.
Chow Chow, 10c.   Sweet Pickles, 10c.   Lettuce, 10c.

PIE.

Pumpkin................................... 10
Mince, Hot or Cold......................... 10
Cranberry................................. 10
Green Apple............................... 05

PUDDING.

English Plum Pudding with Hard and Brandy Sauce.. 10

ICES.

Nougatine Ice Cream........................ 10
Lady Fingers, 10c.   Sponge Cake, 1.   Jelly Roll, 5c.
Macaroons, 10c

FRUIT.

Apples, 10c.   Bananas, 10c.   Oranges, 10c.

DESSERT.

Roqueford Cheese, 10c.   Cream Cheese, 10c.
Bent's Water Crackers, 5c.   Edam Cheese, 10c.
Assorted Nuts and Raisins, 10c.   Black Coffee and Cognac, 15c

Tacoma, Washington's Hotel Chilberg's restaurant offered an extensive New Year's Day menu in 1894. Menu categories included oysters, soup, fish, boiled meats, entrees, game, poultry, roasts, vegetables, cold dishes and salads, relishes, pie, pudding, ices, fruit, and dessert, which included cheese, nuts, coffee, and cognac. COURTESY OF THE NEW YORK PUBLIC LIBRARY

The Florence Hotel in Missoula, Montana, offered a bill of fare for its 1900 New Year's Day dinner. They served mulligatawny, chicken salad *en* mayonnaise, tenderloin of sole, potatoes julienne, breakfast bacon with wax beans, haunch of venison with currant jelly, and escalloped tomatoes. Correctionville, Iowa's *Sioux Valley News* offered a menu option that included julienne soup, browned potatoes, Yorkshire pudding, roast beef, celery salad, apple pudding, and fruits, nuts, and cheese, along with coffee. Even

In 1895 the Portland Hotel offered a decadent menu for the New Year. Selections included green turtle soup with champagne, striped bass, quail with truffles, eggnog, mince pie, and assorted cakes. COURTESY OF THE NEW YORK PUBLIC LIBRARY

places like Donoher's in Valentine, Nebraska, offered oyster soup, lake trout, turkey with dressing, goose, short ribs of beef with chili sauce, oyster patties, banana fritters, mashed and sweet potatoes, Spanish-style stewed tomatoes, French peas, mince and pumpkin pies, strawberry sherbet, cheese, coffee and tea at five o'clock.

Residents of Ukiah, California, ushered in 1908 with ringing bells and blowing horns, even in the rain. Despite the inclement weather, a good-size crowd remained until midnight to ring in the New Year. Watch parties were held in homes, where children were allowed to stay up way past their usual bedtimes. St. John's Church held its usual watch party, while children marched in the muddy streets blowing and ringing their New Year's Eve noisemakers. The Hotel Cecile, known for its superior meals, prepared a holiday feast for New Year's Eve. The *Ukiah Daily Journal* wrote, "The Hotel Cecile has long since established a reputation second to none in entertaining its guests, and when it was made known that a special dinner was to be served on New Year's evening, there was a rush made by the bon vivants of this city to engage tables for the occasion, and to enjoy viands that the Cecile chef would prepare for their enjoyment."

Not only did the hotel offer a special New Year's Eve meal, they decked the restaurant out to match the meal. Their large dining room was decorated with holly berries, evergreens, and clusters of electric lights that "cast a flow of cheerfulness over the throngs of merry diners." The entertainment included a

People often sent warm wishes, inquired about health, and shared brief news of home on the back of these cards (ca. 1900s). SHERRY MONAHAN

FIRST FOOTING

The Scottish people living in Portland, Oregon, held a New Year's Day celebration that was commonly held in their country. It was called Hogmanay. The *Sunday Oregonian* reported,

> *"Altmeal" cakes, "shortie," and "n'er dry bun" are being baked, haggis is being prepared, and the stock of mountain dew increased. Hogmanay means (in Scotch) the time elapsing between the dying on the old year and the birth of the new—a joyous, happy time in which you visit on "first-foot" your intimate friends, carrying seasonable gifts and wishing them a "guid" or happy New Year. In more than one bakery on Third street are cakes of "shortie" or shortbread, with these written in sugar, "Land o' the loal," "Should auld acquaintance be forgot?" "A guid New Year tae ane and a'," and others. These cakes have been baked mostly for Hogmanay people or first-footers.*

They proceeded to explain that the origin of the word: "Hogmanay dates far back into remote history—about the time when it is supposed the canny Scotchman was one of the Kings of Israel. It was a time of boisterous merry-making, of house to house carousals, when women were often kissed and embraced by unwelcome swains, and they cried, 'Hug me nay.' Tradition tells this is how the ancient word Hogmanay was coined."

The Scots in Portland, Oregon, weren't the only ones enjoying Highland traditions. In 1895 Omaha, Nebraska's local paper reported on the social events for the New Year. Mr. and Mrs. Dixon hosted a dancing party, the South Side Skating Club held their party at Spoon Lake near Council Bluffs, and Fort Omaha held their traditional regimental bachelor mess. Mrs. Graham Park hosted a "Scotch Tea" that included Scotch-themed items including broiled beef, ham, and scones and "oat cakes wi' a wee bit o' cheese, shortbread, currant buns, and other distinctively Scotch unpronounceables, received direct from the old country."

string orchestra of six pieces that played strains from *La Boheme* and *Carmen* as well as dreamy waltzes.

As part of the Hotel Cecile's meal, elegant souvenir menus were created for the 150 diners. Some of the items they enjoyed included Eastern oysters, cream of asparagus soup, crab *en* mayonnaise, ham with champagne sauce, stuffed bell peppers, chicken fricassee, tenderloin of beef larded with mushrooms, pineapple fritters, prime rib, Peking duck, suckling pig, turkey, and potatoes and vegetables. To finish the meal, they offered diners English plum pudding, cream puffs, ice cream, cheese, nuts, tea, coffee, chocolate, and mince, lemon cream, and pumpkin pies.

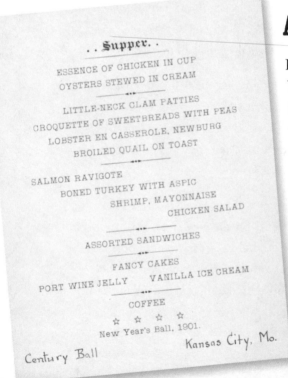

.. Supper ..

ESSENCE OF CHICKEN IN CUP
OYSTERS STEWED IN CREAM

LITTLE-NECK CLAM PATTIES
CROQUETTE OF SWEETBREADS WITH PEAS
LOBSTER EN CASSEROLE, NEWBURG
BROILED QUAIL ON TOAST

SALMON RAVIGOTE
BONED TURKEY WITH ASPIC
SHRIMP, MAYONNAISE
CHICKEN SALAD

ASSORTED SANDWICHES

FANCY CAKES
PORT WINE JELLY   VANILLA ICE CREAM

COFFEE
☆ ☆ ☆ ☆
New Year's Ball, 1901.

Century Ball   Kansas City, Mo.

A New New Year's Tradition

Football was becoming a popular event on New Year's Day across the frontier, and in Corning, Iowa, in 1897 it was a balmy fifty degrees and the perfect weather for a football game. Villisca, whose team was made up of college boys who had come home from school, challenged Corning. Corning made the trip to Villisca and won—four goals to none, which is how they kept score back in the day. After the football game, many of these men, and men like them across the West, would get cleaned up, put on their calling clothes, and make visits around town.

This menu is from the Century Ball on New Year's Eve in Kansas City, Missouri, 1901. Items included oysters, clams, sweetbreads, lobster, quail, sandwiches, fancy cakes, and coffee. COURTESY OF THE NEW YORK PUBLIC LIBRARY

A New Year's Poem

"Oh, Promise Me"

Make me a promise, sweet,

That you will keep. I pray—

To be renewed, throughout the year,

Every golden day.

Forswear no whim or while

That conquered me of old,

Nor promise me your smile—

Your passing frown, your foolish
tear—

To temper or withhold.

Forget no tiny dot

Of girlish vanity,

Nor strive for higher thought

Than has enriched your past, so dear

And helpful unto me;

Valentine Democrat, December 31, 1903

Resolutions

As people dined on delightful meals, they often made New Year's resolutions that were popular in the nineteenth century. The *Great Bend Tribune* in Kansas published some in 1910 from local men who were "overheard" stating theirs. They included the following:

➤ I am tempted to forsake my old friend, the oldest and best known traveling man on the road, but have not fully decided yet.

➤ No spats of any kind for me next year. My cheery countenance will wear the smile that won't come off and I'll always be happy.

➤ I need recreation so I think I will take up auto driving this summer. They say there is exhilaration about it.

➤ No dances for me in 1910. I've been dancing so hard lately that I've callous places all over my feet.

➤ I intend to stay at home from the ball games this summer. Nobody keeps a New Year's resolution anyway and that's the oldest chestnut I can think of.

GAMES WERE ALSO PLAYED ON NEW YEAR'S EVE AND DAY. The card games hearts, whist, and euchre were popular, as were guessing games. Another popular game was called "perception," and it tested a guest's senses.

 ## TO PLAY PERCEPTION

Choose from one to five senses to test party guests.

➤ FOR SIGHT: Arrange items on a tray that is kept out of sight. Bring the items to the participants and allow them to look for one to two minutes. Take the tray away and ask them to write down everything they saw on a sheet of paper. The one who names the most items wins.

➤ FOR HEARING: Select some musical instrument or other sounds to play. Either blindfold or turn off the lights while each sound is made. The player who identifies the most correct sounds wins a prize.

➤ FOR TASTE: Select a set number of beverages, fruit, vegetables, and so on. Blindfold each guest and have them taste. The person who gets the most right wins a prize.

➤ FOR SMELL: Select items with a distinct scent, such as a fresh orange, perfume, vinegar, and so on. Have each guest smell the items. The person who gets the most right wins a prize.

➤ FOR TOUCH: Select items for your guests to touch, like cotton balls, grapes, rice, coins, buttons, and so on. Either hide them in a paper bag or blindfold your guests. The person who gets the most right wins a prize.

New Years' Recipes

The following recipes will liven up any watch party or New Year's Day celebration. These recipes come straight from the menus of the great New Year's celebrations in homes and the best hotels throughout the West in the late nineteenth and early twentieth centuries.

EGGNOG

SERVES 1–2

3 eggs, separated

1 cup plus 1 tablespoon confectioners' sugar

1½ cups cream

¼ teaspoon nutmeg

⅛ cup each brandy and rum

Eggnog was a popular holiday beverage served all over the frontier. SHERRY MONAHAN

Beat the egg yolks and 1 cup confectioners' sugar together in a bowl and set aside. Beat the egg whites with 1 tablespoon confectioners' sugar until stiff peaks form; refrigerate.

Heat the cream and nutmeg in a medium saucepan over medium-high heat and bring just to a boil, stirring occasionally. Remove from the heat and gradually add the hot cream into the egg-and-sugar mixture.

Return everything to the saucepan and cook until the mixture reaches 160°F. Remove from the heat and place in a bowl; set in the refrigerator to chill. Fold the egg whites into the egg mixture and combine. Serve with grated cinnamon and nutmeg.

Note: Caution is advised when consuming raw eggs, so be sure to cook the yolks to 160°F.

Recipe adapted from the *Idaho Daily Statesman*, 1892

LOBSTER SALAD

SERVES 2-3

2 cups lobster, cooked and chopped fine

¼ teaspoon freshly ground pepper

¼ cup lettuce, shredded

½ teaspoon mustard

½ teaspoon salt

½ cup mayonnaise

Lettuce leaves, for plating

Toast points, for plating (see Note)

Place all the ingredients in a large bowl, except for the lettuce and toast points, and combine well. Serve on a bed of lettuce with toast points.

Note: To make toast points, toast slices of bread and cut into triangles.

Recipe adapted from the *Idaho Daily Statesman*, 1892

SARATOGA CHIPS

SERVES 2-4

4 white potatoes

Hot oil or lard

Salt

Slice the unpeeled potatoes thinly and soak in water overnight. The next day, drain and completely dry them. Any water will cause the grease to explode or pop.

Place enough oil in a dutch oven to come up halfway. Heat to medium high. Gently add the potatoes in small batches and fry until golden. Place on paper towels to drain. Sprinkle with salt while still hot.

Recipe adapted from the *Monday Club Cookbook*, Astoria, Oregon, 1899

BROWNED POTATOES

SERVES 4

10–12 small new potatoes, scrubbed

¼ cup butter, melted

½ teaspoon salt

¼ teaspoon freshly ground pepper

Place the potatoes in a baking dish and drizzle the melted butter over them.

Sprinkle with the salt and pepper.

Bake at 375°F for 20 to 30 minutes, or until tender.

Browned potatoes were a popular item served on the frontier for holidays. SHERRY MONAHAN

Recipe adapted from Omaha, Nebraska's *Sunday World Herald*, 1899

YORKSHIRE PUDDING

SERVES 6–10

3 large eggs

1 cup all-purpose flour

¾ cup whole milk

½ teaspoon salt

Vegetable oil or beef drippings

Combine the eggs and flour in a large mixing bowl and beat for 5 minutes.

Gradually add the milk and salt, and beat until combined.

Allow the batter to rest for an hour.

Preheat the oven to 425°F.

Place 1 tablespoon oil into the desired number of cups in a muffin/cupcake pan and put in the oven for about 10 minutes.

Remove the pan from the oven and add 3 to 4 tablespoons batter to each cup.

Bake for 15 to 20 minutes, or until golden.

Remove the puddings from the pan and set them on paper towels to drain for a minute or two.

Serve hot.

Recipe adapted from Montana's *Butte Weekly Miner*, 1897

MULLIGATAWNY

SERVES 4-6

¼ cup butter or margarine

1 cup chicken, diced

¼ cup onion, chopped

¼ cup carrot, chopped

¼ cup celery, chopped

1 green pepper, diced

¼ cup flour

Sprig of fresh parsley

½ teaspoon ground mace

2 whole cloves

1 teaspoon ground turmeric

½ teaspoon salt

⅛ teaspoon freshly ground pepper

1 cup tomatoes, diced

1 apple, diced

4 cups chicken stock

Steamed rice, for serving

Melt the butter in a large pot. Sauté the chicken, onion, carrot, celery, and pepper in the butter over medium-high heat until lightly brown. Add the flour and spices and stir well. Next, add the tomatoes, apples, and chicken stock; simmer for 40 minutes. Taste for seasoning and adjust with salt and pepper. Serve with steamed rice.

Recipe adapted from the Grand Forks, North Dakota's *Daily Herald*, 1908

ESCALLOPED TOMATOES

SERVES 4

1 pint fresh tomatoes, peeled and chopped

1 teaspoon salt

1 teaspoon freshly ground black pepper

1 teaspoon sugar

3 tablespoons butter, melted

½ pint bread crumbs, grated

Mix tomatoes, salt, pepper, sugar, and 2 tablespoons butter, and pour into a baking dish. Sprinkle the bread crumbs over the mixture and drizzle with the remaining 1 tablespoon butter. Bake at 350°F for 30 minutes.

Recipe courtesy of *Kansas City Times*, 1895

SHORTBREAD

SERVES 4-6

½ cup plus 1 tablespoon confectioners' sugar

½ cup plus 1 tablespoon granulated sugar

1¼ cups butter, room temperature

3½ cups all-purpose flour

Preheat the oven to 280°F.

In a large mixing bowl, cream the confectioners' sugar, granulated sugar, and butter together with a wooden spoon.

In another smaller bowl, sift the flour twice and slowly add it to the butter and sugar. Use your hands to mix it well until a firm dough forms.

Lightly flour a work surface and roll or press the dough to a ½-inch thickness. Use a cookie cutter to make rounds or slice it into 3 x 1-inch bars and prick the top with a fork.

Bake for 30 to 40 minutes, or until the shortbread is a light golden color.

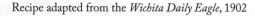

Recipe adapted from the *Wichita Daily Eagle*, 1902

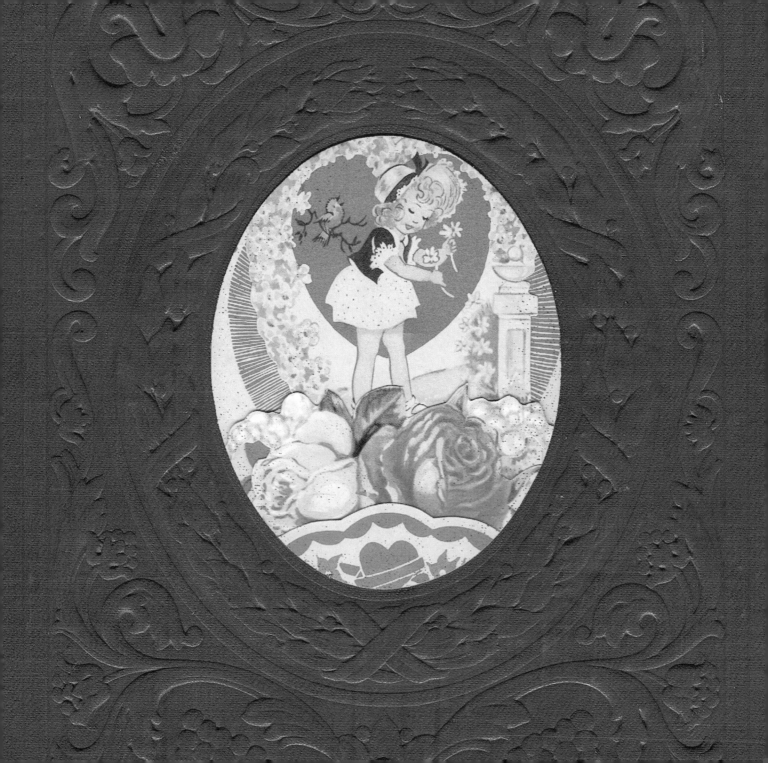

CHAPTER TWO

ST. VALENTINE'S DAY

———————⌗———————

WHEN YOUNG EDWARD MCILHANY LEFT HIS WEST VIRGINIA HOME for the gold fields of California in 1849, he also left behind his sweetheart, the young widow Mrs. Ellen Marshall. Like many young men who headed West alone in search of fortune, he retained warm thoughts of the home he left behind and wrote often to his loved ones. For one Valentine's Day he sent a special—anonymous—gift to his beloved. He recalled, "During my stay in California I had sent her a valentine and a ring, a beautiful ring made out of California gold. I did not attach any name." She never knew who sent the ring until after he returned to West Virginia. He later recalled:

> *I asked her if she received a valentine from California. She said she received one, and it was beautiful, no name attached to it, but she, with others, believed I had sent it. "Your picture I got in Washington City and I have it put away in my trunk to keep it from being soiled and destroyed, and I take it out and look at it often. Not knowing for certain who sent the ring to me, I let Miss Jennie Marbury have it to wear until I could ascertain who sent it." She wrote a note immediately to Miss Jennie that I had returned and for her to send the ring back immediately as I was the one who sent it, and she dispatched a negro servant with the note. She received the ring in a short time. In*

the presence of the family of her husband she said, "I will now wear this ring as long as I live as I know who sent it."

St. Valentine's Day, as it was almost universally called in the nineteenth century, was celebrated across the country by Victorians who mailed cards, letters, and gifts to their sweethearts and loved ones. For those who went to the frontier and left their loved ones behind, St. Valentine's Day was also an excellent chance to send a special message about how much they missed one another.

Another young man reached out from the California's gold fields on February 14, 1850. Enos Christman penned a Valentine letter to his fiancée back home. The printer's apprentice had been away from his beloved Ellen Apple since June the previous year, when he'd left friends and family behind in West Chester, Pennsylvania, to seek his fortune with the gold seekers in California:

> *Betrothed Ellen—This day a year ago, I little dreamed that in a twelvemonth I should have encountered the terrors of Cape Horn, and after many days of severe suffering, reached the shores of this golden land, and been penning you an epistle like this. But strange as this would have sounded then, it is now nevertheless true. . . . In order to perpetuate the good old custom of sending letters of love and friendship on St. Valentine's Day, I must write a short letter of friendship to Miss Hunter. Were you of a less generous disposition, I should hardly dare to tell you this, but I know you are not blinded by the foolish and jealous passions so often found in your sex. I know you will never allow yourself to be disturbed by the petty reports often found floating through the community and always added to by busy mischief-makers. But believe me, I would rather that the hand which now guides my pen should wither than deceive you in this. And if you feel the least disturbed on this account you can apply to me for a copy of this letter, which I will forward you if you desire it.*

One hopes he also had a happy outcome from his honest and heartfelt letter.

While Valentine's Day celebrations are primarily considered a romantic couples holiday, men, women, and children also celebrated the day in the 1800s. Many people held private residence parties, while others had large public celebrations at hotels and other locations. Hostesses decorated their homes with red and pink cupids and hearts with arrows. Churches, lodges, hotels, and private individuals held St. Valentine's Day parties, too. Whether together or apart, pioneers on the western frontier carried on the tradition of celebrating St. Valentine's Day in ways similar to today's celebrations.

The Valentine

To honor St. Valentine's Day, the young and old alike sent cards to family members, secret loves, sweethearts, and even teachers. This was also a day when people would take time to send letters to friends, letting them know they were thinking of them. Men worried about sending the proper card or gift, and girls fantasized about receiving a valentine from the man of her dreams. Their big decision was whether to send a serious, romantic, or a comic one. Making the wrong choice could definitely send the wrong message!

Rhyming St. Valentine's Day cards were very common during the nineteenth century. Valentine's cards were simply referred to as a valentine—meaning a card.

A typical romantic valentine postcard (ca. 1900s). SHERRY MONAHAN

By the 1860s, stationery companies were making preprinted valentines, and many were bought and sent. It was not uncommon for some lovers to include fancy gifts in their cards. In the Portland *Daily Oregonian* in 1869, a local merchant, McCormick's, ran an advertisement offering one hundred gross of comical valentines and fifty thousand sentimental valentines. Prices ranged from $0.25 to $150.00.

San Francisco's children and adults fully embraced St. Valentine's Day in 1865, and the city delivered over ten thousand valentines. That number didn't include the ones that were delivered by local valentine card merchants, who sold them and handled private deliveries.

Most adult St. Valentine's Day cards were pretty, with flowers and lace, but those for children had a different look, feel, and purpose. There was a cute custom for children to send funny valentines to a friend or loved one. Over time, the custom was practiced by adults as well. In the mid-1860s, the *Dallas Weekly Herald* wrote,

The relation that this day had to St. Valentine has long been forgotten. It used to be a practice for gentlemen and ladies to consider the first one they met on this day as their lover or Valentine, and the meeting was usually followed by an interchange of presents. Afterwards it became custom for young folks on that day to interchange anonymous letters, often accompanied with humorous and quizzical pictures. In this country it has become to be a day in which friends of all ages and sexes are at liberty, or take the liberty of interchanging ridiculous pictures—the most so the better—in pretense of ridiculing or burlesquing some peculiar trait of character in the person to whom it is sent. Nothing offensive is ever intended, but rather a presumption of the most intimate relations or cordial friendship; and no one takes offense at anything received, or predicated on that day.

Frey's store on Kearny Street in San Francisco offered a variety of valentines in 1875. They included valentines that were perfumed with twelve different flowers, embossed and trimmed with lace and gold, in boxes with artificial flowers, English-style in oval boxes, comics "of every conceivable description," and jeweled boxes.

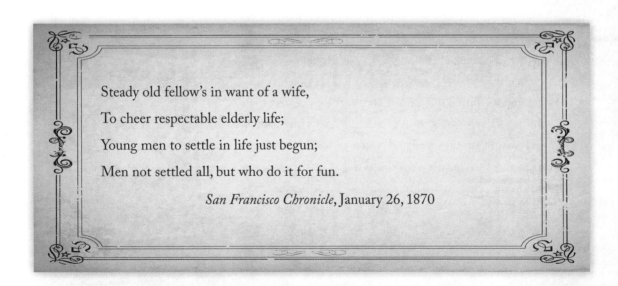

Steady old fellow's in want of a wife,

To cheer respectable elderly life;

Young men to settle in life just begun;

Men not settled all, but who do it for fun.

San Francisco Chronicle, January 26, 1870

The year 1864 was a special one for the Victorian ladies: It was leap year. During this special year, the young maidens were allowed to break protocol and send their sweethearts cards and gifts.

In 1894, the *Dallas Morning News* reported, "We are not limited to the old-fashioned lace valentine, such as your grandmother can show in its embossed and yellowed envelope, although you may buy exactly such a one, for the call for this style never seems to grow less. Perhaps the only valentine that is really on the wane is the so-called 'comic' valentine, which however, is seldom very funny, but always vulgar." Another option was to send a gift but no card at all. If one was skipping the card, then the gift should be in a heart shape. The newspaper recommended a heart-shaped calendar for women and a handmade, monogramed tobacco pouch for men, suggesting women use a pair of their own kid gloves to make the pouch. An additional gift idea for men was a handmade heart-shaped frame with his sweetheart's photo inside. Yet another story stated that sending flowers was a graceful and pleasing way to make a lady happy on this special day. It was suggested that an engaged man offer his fiancée jewelry if he had money or a pretty heart-shaped mirror if his bank account was small. Other gift suggestions included an inkstand and gold pen or some fancy ink blotters.

A funny, romantic valentine postcard (ca. 1900s).
SHERRY MONAHAN

THE LANGUAGE OF FLOWERS

MANY VICTORIAN PIONEERS PAID CLOSE ATTENTION to which flower they chose to send because they all carried very different meaning. Those living in rural areas relied on what they grew in their gardens or what grew wild around them. It was also important when choosing which flowers appeared on one's written valentine. A nineteenth-century book called *The Language of Flowers* contained a list of flowers and their meanings. Imagine getting a valentine flower or card with an African marigold. That flower's meaning equals vulgar minds. An azalea meant temperance, while a buttercup implied ingratitude or childishness. The poor lover who received those valentines must have been sad that February 14. Better choices included forget-me-nots, which denoted true love; honeysuckles signified generous and devoted affection; and a single pink carnation meant pure love. The rose? There were so many varieties of roses, and their meanings included purity, devotion, and love. Violets were all the rage, according to the local florists, and were packed in wicker or grass baskets. In the language of flowers, violets signified faithfulness, which also made them popular.

The language of flowers was of great importance for Victorians and many knew the meaning for most flowers by heart. A Grand Forks, North Dakota, newspaper printed a story called "What Flowers Tell," and it included a list of the best known flowers:

Sweet alyssum = worth beyond beauty

Apple blossom = preference, or will you be mine?

Bachelor's button = single and selfish

Balm = sympathy

Barberry = sourness

Candytuft = indifference

Pink carnation = woman's love

Chinese chrysanthemum = cheerfulness under misfortune

Clematis = mental clarity

Columbine = folly

Red clover = industry

Dahlia = dignity

White daisy = innocence

Faded leaves = melancholy

Forget-me-not = remembrance

Jonquil = affections returned

Lily of the valley = return of happiness

Pansy = you occupy my thoughts

Moss rose = I am worthy of love

Sunflower = haughtiness

Yellow rose = infidelity

Courtesy of the *Daily Herald*, December 10, 1892

Candy Valentines

It wasn't until around 1895 that candy started being associated with Cupid's day. One company in Kansas City, Missouri, advertised, "So pretty and dainty. Those valentine candy boxes at Morton's. Individual heart ice cream moulds for valentine parties."

In 1866 Oliver Chase of Boston invented "conversation candies," which are known today as Sweetheart candies—those heart-shaped candies with romantic sentiments stamped on them. They were originally all white and called lozenges.

By 1902 trends in candy had shifted, and some people didn't like what was being printed on the candy lozenge. The headline and story in Kansas's *Iola Daily Register* read, "Latest in Slang Candy. Some of the verbal trash that has supplanted the old sentimental inscriptions." The report went on:

> *Do you remember the old-fashioned, flat, scalloped, diamond, or heart-shaped candy lozenge, ornamented with sentimental words, such as, "Sweetheart," "My Own True Love," "Faithful to Thee," "Ever Thine," and so on? We used to pass these around at little gatherings when I was young, and much harmless but deeply fervent love-making was carried on by all means of such simple tokens. The pink and white candy lozenge of the present day, however, is a degenerate. It is much smaller in size, although still scalloped, and the phrases stamped on its surface are below the dignity of genteel members of the lozenge family. The words you read now on the candy lozenges are as follows: "That's What," "My Best Girl," "Rubberneck," "Move On," "Bat Them Out," "My Size," "Do*

You Bike?" "Gee Whiz," "My Baby Lou," "Guess Not," "Just So," "Come Again," "That Face," and so on.

After the turn of the century, chocolate and candy started making their way into St. Valentine's Day as serious gifts. In 1903, the *Seattle Daily Times* printed a story that reflected the change in St. Valentine's Day gifts. The old custom of sending laced-edges cards with tender sentiments had been replaced with elaborate floral designs and expensive candy boxes that included valentine designs and sentiments. The *Seattle Daily Sunday* paper reported, "Candy is a favorite gift for St. Valentine's Day. The young man whose fate is underdetermined is more apt to send flowers which breathe his sentiments—for it is all the fashion now to send with their sentiments—but the young man whose future is settled by a solitaire diamond ring will send his fiancée one of the boxes of candy especially got up for the day."

Candy boxes came in many sizes, from a foot and half across to a tiny red heart with a cupid sitting atop a spray of orange blossoms or lilies of the valley. The boxes were all heart shaped and made of satin or brocaded silk. They were hand-painted with spring blossoms on the top or embroidered with small wreaths and sprays. They were adorned with embroidered ribbons and later repurposed for glove boxes, jewel cases, and other items. The candy was tucked into the folds of satin, and lace lined the box. Each contained a suitable verse or sentiment of lithographed valentines.

Two years later newspaper ads for candy-filled valentine boxes were seen in newspapers. Chocolates, bonbons, caramels, and buttercups were very popular. The *Kansas City Star* contained one that offered heart-shaped boxes filled with candy for five cents. Cornelius's candy store also offered "heart-shaped boxes, lovely, filled with choice chocolates, etc. 1 lb. each . . . 35 c." In 1909 a Denver, Colorado, candy store advertised a full line of heart-shaped mints, in a variety of flavors and colors for thirty-five cents per pound. Thus began the current association of chocolate and Valentine's Day.

Celebrations

Many local newspapers included ideas for decorating and what to serve for valentine luncheons and dinners. For a luncheon the *Kansas City* (Missouri) *Times* suggested this for Valentine's Day in 1895:

> *Have everything rose-colored, with decorations of hearts, horseshoes, love knots, and the like. . . . A heart-shaped center piece made of pink roses with a silver or gold dart stuck through it will be found effective. Other pretty ideas for table decorations are center designs of hearts done in carnations, forget-me-nots, or violet ties with love knots of corresponding colored ribbons. At each place have a bunch of roses caught with pink ribbon, and having a pink enamel arrow tied in the bow. . . . If you have pink china it will be found effective. It is no trick at all to have a roll at each place in the shape of a horseshoe. Bakers are clever nowadays and will do it for one. For the menu card use heart-shaped pink cardboard or vellum tinted that color. The name of the guest and date will occupy one side of the cards and the menu the other. If you like, a quotation apropos to each guest can be added under the name. Some of the following may furnish hints:*

> *None knew thee but to love thee, None name thee but to praise. —Halleck*

> *But to see her was to love her, Love but her and her forever. —Burns*

> *No I am in a holiday humor. —Shakespeare*

For valentine dinners, they offered these "colorful" ideas if the guest was a man:

> *If you are entertaining men—and what is a valentine dinner without the sterner sex—give them something to eat. This may sound odd, but one hears many a wail of woe from masculine lips over the average girl's idea of a dinner. "It is worse than a frothy glass*

of soda water," said an abused bachelor lately, "for even at the end there is nothing." So include at least one substantial course in the menu—try beef. There is no denying it, men like beef.

The article continued:

Caviar on heart-shaped pieces of toast is a good commencement, followed by cream of love-apple soup ("love apples" is the name tomatoes often go by). Twin soles make an excellent fish course. Two good-sized flounders will be sufficient for a small dinner, and the name sole often applied to them. For an entrée sweetbreads. Fillet of beef with mushrooms may be made to look quite apropos by a little culinary decoration. Have the pieces of fillet cut thick, and on the top of each lay a piece of thin sliced beef cut heart-shaped; serve the mushrooms around it. For game turtle doves, on ordinary occasions known as squabs, will be appropriate. Serve celery in heart-shaped cases. Ice cream can be molded into any shape—hearts, love-knots, roses or horseshoes being equally pretty, and kisses are substituted for cake. Use the heart-shaped peppermints with sentimental verses which "go" on St. Valentines' day for bonbons.

Name the Author: Give each guest a pen and sheet of paper. Have then write an anonymous valentine message and fold the paper. Place all messages in a bowl and draw one a time. The guests try to guess the name of the author. Have small valentine-related prizes for the winners.

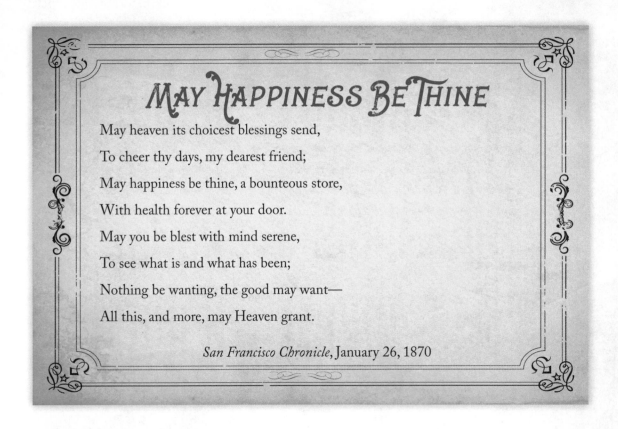

MAY HAPPINESS BE THINE

May heaven its choicest blessings send,

To cheer thy days, my dearest friend;

May happiness be thine, a bounteous store,

With health forever at your door.

May you be blest with mind serene,

To see what is and what has been;

Nothing be wanting, the good may want—

All this, and more, may Heaven grant.

San Francisco Chronicle, January 26, 1870

A Valentine's Day Tree

The *Dallas Morning News* ran a woman's column written under the pen name, Little Miss Big Bonnet, or "Little Miss." In February 1897, Little Miss wrote about a Valentine's Day tree. During a past Christmas Little Miss had whooping cough and couldn't go see the Christmas tree lighting in town. She was very sad, indeed, so her mother suggested she have a St. Valentine's evening party. At her party, her mother placed a live tree on the

Valentine: Give each guest a pen and sheet of paper with the word *Valentine* written on it. Have them create as many whole words as possible in a designated time frame. Have small valentine-related prizes for the winner.

---

parlor table. Little Miss recalled, "We got a tree just like a little fat, bunchy Christmas tree. It stood on the table in the middle of the parlor, and had beautiful lighted candles and bright ornaments on it." She invited her friends and placed a valentine for each one of them on the tree. In proper fashion, she was treated to eleven of her own valentines from her guests. For supper, they snacked on heart-shaped sandwiches, cakes, and candy hearts.

A Bit of Holiday Cynicism

St. Valentine's Day was being adulterated by the use of comic valentines. According to North Dakota's *Bismarck Tribune* in 1890, St. Valentine's Day, not all was rosy in the celebration of the holiday. The reporter called the story, "How Abuse Kills a Custom." It stated,

> *That St. Valentine's day observances began by reason of man's observation of nature, continued as matter of sentiment, and finally degenerated into mere fun, is known to all well-informed persons, and is, in fact, true of nearly all social customs. . . . Signs of coming spring were apparent at that season, and so the birds were thought to choose their mates of the year on that date. Simple, innocent notion, wasn't it? . . . At first*

Fortune-Telling: Before guests arrive, write some funny or sweet fortunes on sheets of paper—enough for each guest and the host and/or hostess. Have each guest draw the fortune from a heart-shaped container and have them read their fortune aloud.

youths and maidens chose their partners ("valentines") on that day for approaching festivities and little presents were sent to loved ones. But in no long time the great began to expect costly presents from their dependents. . . . In the United States the abuse first took the form of ill-natured satire . . . though "comic valentines" are still used, they are externally quite different from the sentimental ones, and are usually treated with silent contempt. . . . Valentines are now left to children and servants, and even with them the sentiment has mostly given place to merriment. As to sending a "comic," a lady or gentleman would as soon think of stealing a sheep. The law also stepped in; Uncle Sam says you must not use his mails for a scurrilous valentine. So the custom must die out for a while—to revive in the future, as other customs have done.

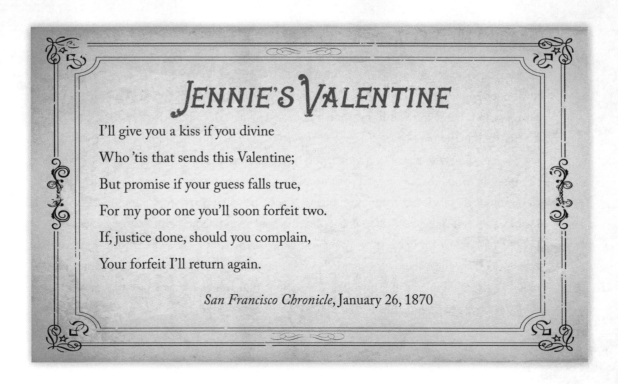

JENNIE'S VALENTINE

I'll give you a kiss if you divine

Who 'tis that sends this Valentine;

But promise if your guess falls true,

For my poor one you'll soon forfeit two.

If, justice done, should you complain,

Your forfeit I'll return again.

San Francisco Chronicle, January 26, 1870

Conundrums: Come up with valentine-related theme words, such as Cupid, sweetheart, candy, roses, and so on. Scramble the letters for each word and post them around the area where your guests will be able to see them. Give each guest a pen and sheet of paper and have them write down the unscrambled word. Whoever gets the most correct words wins. Have small valentine-related prizes for the winner.

Recipes for a Pioneer St. Valentine's Day

These recipes and food are suggested by the Victorian pioneers themselves, printed in local newspapers. The *Duluth News Tribune* suggested fried chicken with Spanish tomato sauce, potato balls, and cauliflower au gratin, as well as a decadent dessert, for a Valentine's dinner menu. The *Fort Worth Telegram* suggested St. Valentine's canapés, cheese sandwiches, crown roast of lamb, heart-shaped potatoes, and peas in white sauce. Other recipes include foods that are white, red and pink, are made into heart shapes, or are thought to be romantic of some nature. Some tasty Valentine's Day party foods included chicken timbales served in heart-shaped cups, heart-shaped sandwiches, chicken salad served in a heart-shaped ring, and cheese straws shaped into arrows. For the sweet tooth there were cranberry tarts and small heart-shaped cakes that were tinted with red color. Hot chocolate was also a popular drink to serve. The recipes that follow are from newspapers all over the West and are included to verify what the pioneers were eating.

TOMATO SOUP

SERVES 4

2 tablespoons butter

1 carrot, peeled and sliced

1 turnip, peeled and sliced

1 onion, peeled and sliced

1 stalk celery, sliced

4 tablespoons flour

4 cups beef or vegetable broth

1 (28-ounce) can tomatoes or 3 cups fresh tomatoes, chopped

1 bay leaf

Pinch of freshly grated nutmeg

½ teaspoon salt

⅛ teaspoon freshly ground pepper

Croutons, for garnish

Melt the butter in a large pot. Cook the carrot, turnip, onion, and celery in the butter over medium-high heat. When the mixture is golden, stir in the flour. Cook for an additional 2 minutes. Add the remaining ingredients (except the croutons) and bring to a boil. Reduce the heat to low and cook until all the vegetables are tender. Force the mixture through a sieve, or puree and strain. Season to taste with salt and pepper.

Return the pot to the stove and bring the soup to a boil. Serve warm with croutons sprinkled on top.

Note: To reduce the acidity in this recipe, dissolve 1 teaspoon of baking soda in 2 tablespoons of water. Pour this in the soup after you have reduced the heat.

Recipe adapted from the *California Farmer*, 1867

CHICKEN SALAD

SERVES 2

2 cups cooked chicken, cut into small pieces

½ cup celery, diced

¼–½ cup Homemade Mayonnaise (recipe follows)

Lettuce leaves

Capers (optional), for garnish

Combine chicken with the celery and mayonnaise, and stir to combine. Place a scoop of the salad on a lettuce leaf and garnish with a few capers. Use heart-shaped plates.

HOMEMADE MAYONNAISE

MAKES APPROXIMATELY 2 CUPS

1 hard-boiled egg yolk

1 raw egg yolk

½ teaspoon salt

Dash of cayenne pepper

2 teaspoons apple cider vinegar

½ teaspoon yellow mustard

1½ teaspoons lemon juice

2 cups oil

Combine the eggs in a bowl and whip well. Add the salt, cayenne pepper, vinegar, mustard, and lemon juice. Slowly add the oil, drop by drop, while beating the entire time. Do this until the oil is gone and you have a smooth, creamy mayonnaise.

Note: Substitute premade mayonnaise, but add the mustard and taste the salad for seasoning. Adjust with salt and cayenne pepper.

Recipes adapted from Omaha, Nebraska's *World Herald*, 1895

RED CAKE

MAKES 1 CAKE

⅔ cup butter

2 cups sugar

1 teaspoon vanilla

8 drops red food coloring

6 egg whites, beaten

2½ cups flour

2 level teaspoons baking powder

1 cup milk

Fluffy Icing (recipe follows)

In a large bowl combine the butter and sugar and whip until light and fluffy.

Add the vanilla and food coloring.

Beat the egg whites using an electric mixer until stiff peaks form; set aside.

Combine the flour and baking powder in a small bowl. Alternately add the flour mixture and milk to the butter and sugar, beginning and ending with flour, beating until mixed.

Gently fold in the egg whites and mix until combined.

Pour into a greased 11 x 14-inch pan and bake at 350°F for 30 to 35 minutes, or until done. Check with a toothpick.

Frost with Fluffy Icing.

FLUFFY ICING

FROSTS 1 CAKE

2 cups sugar

2 teaspoons lemon juice

⅔ cup water

3 egg whites

Place the sugar, lemon juice, and water into a medium saucepan and bring to a boil. Boil, but do not stir, until the mixture is thick and bubbly and looks like thread if spun from a spoon, 10 to 15 minutes. The liquid will be reduced by half.

Beat the egg whites in a large bowl with a mixer or by hand until stiff peaks form.

When the sugar mixture is ready, gradually add it to the egg whites while beating with a mixer. Whip constantly until stiff peaks form, about 5 to 7 minutes. Allow to cool to room temperature.

Frost cake and decorate for the holiday.

Recipes adapted from St. Louis's *Republic*, May 27, 1900

HOT CHOCOLATE

SERVES 2

½ square of dark chocolate or 1 heaping tablespoon of chocolate chips

1 tablespoon sugar

1 tablespoon hot water

1 cup milk

Place the chocolate, sugar, and water into a saucepan over low heat. Allow the chocolate to slowly melt. Use a whisk to blend until the mixture is smooth and glossy.

Add the milk and allow it to warm, but do not boil. Serve in teacups.

Recipe adapted from *Cocoa and Chocolate: A Short History of Their Production and Use*, 1886

JELLY TARTS

SERVES 6–8

2 cups flour

1 cup cold butter

1 teaspoon salt

½ cup water

Red jelly, for spreading

Combine the flour, butter, and salt, and rub it into a coarse meal. Next add the water and mix only until it turns into a ball of dough. Roll out to an ⅛-inch thickness and cut into hearts. Take half the hearts and cut out a smaller heart in the center. Bake all the hearts in a 350°F oven for 3 to 5 minutes, but do not allow the hearts to brown. Remove them from the oven and allow to cool. Spread the jelly on the whole hearts and top each one with the open hearts so the jelly can be seen through the heart cutout.

Recipe adapted from the *Duluth News Tribune*, 1906

FAIRIES CREAM

MAKES 1 QUART

1 quart heavy cream

1 cup sugar

1 cup candied cherries

Combine the ingredients in a large bowl and stir until the sugar dissolves. Pour into an ice cream maker and follow the manufacturer's instructions to make ice cream. When done, line a cookie sheet with parchment paper and press the ice cream into it. Allow to freeze about 2 hours so that heart shapes can be cut out and served.

Recipe adapted from the *Duluth News Tribune*, 1906

ST. VALENTINE'S CANAPÉS

SERVES 4

½ pound cooked shrimp

⅛ teaspoon cayenne pepper

¼ cup mayonnaise

12 slices firm white bread

Combine the shrimp, cayenne pepper, and mayonnaise in a small bowl and mash them together. Chill until ready to use. Toast the bread until golden brown. Once cooled, cut out the centers with a heart-shaped cutter. Spread a teaspoon of the shrimp spread on each heart. Serve immediately.

Recipe adapted from the *Fort Worth Telegram*, 1904

CHEESE SANDWICHES

MAKES 6 SANDWICHES

2 cups grated Parmesan cheese

1 cup butter

1 teaspoon mustard

Salt and pepper to taste

6 slices white bread

6 slices brown or wheat bread

Mix the cheese, butter, and mustard together in a medium bowl, beating well. Taste for seasoning and add salt and pepper if needed.

Cut out the centers of the bread with a heart-shaped cutter. Take one white heart and one brown heart and spread the cheese filling between the two. Chill or serve at once.

Recipe adapted from *Scammell's Cyclopedia of Valuable Receipts*, 1897

HEART-SHAPED POTATOES

SERVES 4

Butter, for frying

4 large red-skinned potatoes

Salt and pepper to taste

Chopped fresh parsley, for garnish

Heat the butter in a large frying pan over medium-high heat. Slice the potatoes into 1- to 3-inch oval slices. Place a few in the pan at a time, but do not crowd them. Fry on each side until golden browned. Cut into hearts using a heart-shaped cookie cutter. Serve on a platter with some parsley for garnish.

Recipe adapted from the *Fort Worth Telegram*, 1904

CHAPTER THREE

EASTER

⎯⎯⎯⎯⎯⎯⎯⎯⎯⎯ ⚬ ⎯⎯⎯⎯⎯⎯⎯⎯⎯⎯

EASTER ON THE FRONTIER COULD FIND PIONEERS IN WYOMING donning heavy coats, with snow on the ground, or welcoming spring in Southern California. Regardless of the weather, even in the nineteenth century, Easter was a day when children looked forward to colored eggs and bunnies, and pioneers dressed in their finest clothes and hats, attended church services, and had a special meal. Church notices for Easter services and celebrations appeared as prominently as Christmas ads did in December. The church notices included the name of the priest or minister, the songs to be sung, and the special guests brought in to lead the hymns.

The reason for celebrating Easter was a popular newspaper topic across the West. Leavenworth, Kansas's *Times and Conservative* took some space in their 1870 newspaper to explain Easter. They wrote, "Today is Easter Sunday, and for the benefit of those who have never taken the trouble to post themselves on its history, we give below some account. Easter is the festival of the resurrection of the Lord or the Christmas Passover. The English name Easter and the German Ostern are supposed to be derived from the same feast of the Teutonic Goddess, Ostera (the Goddess of spring), which was celebrated by the ancient Saxons in the spring, and for which the early missionaries substituted the

Christian festival." They went on to explain that in nearly all Christian ceremonies, there were popular superstitions. Making colored eggs as presents that were ornately decorated was the most common. Colored eggs were used by children as a game by testing the strength of the egg shells.

This lovely Easter postcard features the letters IHS, *which refers to the Lord (ca. 1900s).* SHERRY MONAHAN

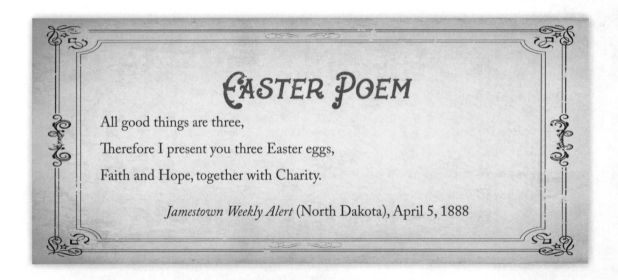

EASTER POEM

All good things are three,

Therefore I present you three Easter eggs,

Faith and Hope, together with Charity.

Jamestown Weekly Alert (North Dakota), April 5, 1888

North Dakota's *Jamestown Weekly Alert* published a story about the custom of Easter eggs for the wee ones. They told the story of a pious queen who sought refuge from her enemies in a remote valley where her poor subjects lived. According to the fable, they had never seen a chicken but knew of eggs. One of her faithful servants began delivering the queen some birds, but the poor had still not seen them. When Easter came, the queen realized she had no gifts to offer the children, so she gathered all the eggs she had and began to color them. She hid them around her garden and invited all the children to search for the concealed treasures. As they searched, one child saw a bunny leap from the vicinity of the nest. The child exclaimed, "Oh, it is a hare that lays the Easter eggs!"

Egg War: Each person has one colored, hard-boiled egg. Use a random way to choose who goes first. The first person is the egg tapper; the remaining participants are called holders. The roles of tapper and holder can change throughout the game. The tapper holds his or her egg with the small end pointing down. The tapper goes to the first egg holder, who holds their egg with the small end up. The holder cannot move while the tapper tries to break the holder's egg. If the tapper's egg remains unbroken and the holder's has a crack, the tapper moves on to the next holder, and so on. If the tapper's egg cracks, the holder becomes the new tapper, and the game continues until the last egg is left. The person with the last remaining uncracked egg wins the game. The winner is declared a "cock of one, two, three, and so on," based on how many eggs they cracked.

AN EASTER IN CALIFORNIA

FORTY-ONE-YEAR-OLD ENGLISHWOMAN Constance Frederica Gordon Cumming sailed from Tahiti to San Francisco, California, in April 1878. She arrived on Easter morning at 2:00 a.m. and later wrote of her time in San Francisco:

There was nothing golden in our first glimpses of California. We indulged in a jorum of excellent hot gin-toddy, to correct the bitter, damp cold; and soon after sunrise we watched a number of huge steamers, densely crowded with excursionists, start from the different wharfs, to make the most of the Easter holiday. Then we made our little preparations for landing. . . . By this time the Easter chimes were pealing from a multitude of church bells, and the streets were thronged with masses of human beings. The grey chill morning was succeeded by a day of brilliant sunlight, and among the crowds of church-goers were many in apparel positively gorgeous. London streets would wonder to find themselves swept by such magnificent satins and velvets, or to see such diamonds glittering in the light of the sun. It struck me painfully to notice the great proportion of women who would evidently have been attractive but for the free use of white and rouge: you might fancy that "this glorious climate of California" could dispense with such polluting adjuncts, but these ladies evidently think otherwise. And yet how they would despise their brown sisters or brothers who on a gala-day "assist nature" by a touch of vermilion or a few streaks of blue! My travelling companion being a rigid Roman Catholic, led the way to St. Mary's Roman Catholic Cathedral, where the bishop was celebrating High Mass. It is a plain building, but made beautiful by its Easter decorations and the profusion of exquisite flowers. Thousands of roses and lilies made the air fragrant, and were doubly welcome to eyes weary of the broad restless ocean. It seemed to me somewhat a strange coincidence that, having received my last *ecclesiastical impressions of the Old World at the Roman Catholic Church of Saint Roch, in Paris, on Good Friday 1875, I should next hear the grand Easter Anthem in a Roman Catholic cathedral on this my first morning in the New World. The singing was most lovely, but the crowd was so dense that there was not a chance of a seat; so, leaving my friend to her devotions, I went to Grace Church—an Episcopal Church which she had pointed out to me a little farther.*

This was likewise densely crowded, but a very civil stranger gave me his seat, for which I was grateful, the walk uphill from the wharf having proved fatiguing. Here also the decorations are most elaborate. Besides the great cross above the altar (made entirely of rare hothouse flowers), there hangs suspended from the great chancel arch an immense cross of pure white Calla lilies (Arum) in a circle of evergreens, beneath which, in very large evergreen letters, each hanging separate, is the angel's Easter greeting—"HE IS RISEN." The effect of this device, so mysteriously floating in mid-air, is very striking. In every corner of the church, flowers have been showered with the same lavish hand—the font, lectern, pulpit, organ, walls, but especially in the chancel, where the choicest flowers are reserved for the altar-vases and the altar-rails, which are altogether hidden by the wealth of exquisite roses. To some sensitive persons, I can imagine that their perfume might have been overpowering, but to me it seemed like a breath from heaven. It was pleasant, too, in this "far country," to hear the old familiar liturgy, like a voice from over the wide waters, bringing with it a flood of home memories and associations. Moreover, it was quite unexpected, as during the last two years I have been thrown in company with so many different regiments of the great Christian army, that I suppose I had assumed that this Californian church would prove one more variety. Certainly, I had not realised that America has preserved the old Book of Common Prayer almost intact, with only a few minor changes.

Flowers and Easter Eggs

As Mrs. Gordon Cumming noted, the floral decorations at the San Francisco church she visited were extensive and impressive. While pioneers in California and Arizona had the luxury of local fresh flowers, however, those living in places where snow was still on the ground had to make do with artificial or dried ones.

Easter decorations were mostly reserved for the churches, but pioneer women did decorate their parlors and dinner tables with floral centerpieces and colored eggs.

Elaborate Easter decorations at St. Paul's Episcopal Church in Benecia, California, 1886. COURTESY OF THE NEW YORK PUBLIC LIBRARY

Fresh eggs were wrapped in colored calico or boiled in dye, and imitation and candy shells were filled with confections or jewelry.

Although some pioneers lived remotely, they still managed to find a way to celebrate Easter. One pioneer mother, Mrs. C. C. West, who lived in Schleicher County, Texas, was desperate for her hen to lay an egg for her son. The family lived under a big live oak tree for six months before they got a tent. She recalled one of her Easters:

While we were living under the big tree, Easter was approaching and the little boy had been told the story of the rabbit's laying for him, etc., until I thought it would be disastrous for Easter to come on and that child without an Easter egg. I had one old dominecker hen and she hadn't laid an egg for weeks but the day before Easter I was prompted to go to her coop and she hadn't failed me. Lying there, all bright and shiny, was a big white egg. It all sounds foolish now, I know, but I was a fond young mother in a strange land and to me that egg was a beautiful sight. Eagerly I snatched it up, ran into the house and began coloring it with my quilt scraps. That was the prettiest Easter egg I have ever seen and of course I have seen every kind since then. The rabbit had been under a tub for days so we all had a very joyful Easter, even if we did have only a live oak tree for a home.

This colorful postcard depicts the Easter bunny delivering the eggs (ca. 1900s). SHERRY MONAHAN

While Mrs. West only had scraps of cloth for egg coloring, others living in towns were able to purchase a well-known twenty-first-century product. Paas egg dye was being sold in packets in the 1880s and was later converted into dye tablets. By 1901 drug stores across the West were selling color and decorating kits. The Strahlmann-Mayer Drug Company in San Diego was one such store and advertised "Easter Eggs for everyone . . . the brilliant dyes we sell furnish kaleidoscopic variations of the primary colors. Dyes sold in packets at five cents each, every shade you can think of."

Easter Dinner

San Diego was, and still is, home to the grand Hotel del Coronado. In 1901 they hosted an Easter dinner that was complete with the most popular entree, which was lamb. In addition to the dinner, the hotel's concert hall offered musical entertainment. Notable guests at the hotel for Easter included the vice president of the Santa Fe Railway and Ford Harvey, son of Fred Harvey and head of the restaurant empire and employer of the Harvey Girl waitresses. Hotels, restaurants, and private homes served lamb with mint sauce and peas, as well as local items they had nearby. Their fare also included oysters, shad, chicken, beef, gosling, puddings, pies, cakes, and more.

Temperature at Noon Today was 62°

HOTEL DEL CORONADO
CORONADO BEACH, CALIFORNIA

E. S. BABCOCK, Manager

DINNER

CANAPE OF ANCHOVIES

CALIFORNIA OYSTER COCKTAIL

BLUE POINTS
OLIVES   MORTADELLA   SWEET PICKLED FIGS   SALTED ALMONDS
CONSOMME NATIONAL   CREAM OF ASPARAGUS, A LA VIENNOISE

BOILED ROCK COD, A LA DUCHESSE
BROILED SHAD, MAITRE D'HOTEL

SLICED TOMATOES   POTATOES DUMAS   STUFFED MANGOES

HAM GLACE, CHAMPAGNE SAUCE

ROAST RIBS OF PRIME BEEF   ROAST SPRING LAMB, MINT SAUCE
ROAST CHICKEN, STUFFED, GIBLET SAUCE

BOILED POTATOES   MASHED POTATOES   GREEN PEAS   SPINACH
ARTICHOKES   COLD ASPARAGUS, FRENCH DRESSING

FILET OF BEEF, LARDED, WITH MUSHROOMS
BROILED GALLINULE, SAUCE ORANGE BIGARRADE
SWEETBREADS EN CASSEROLE, TOULOUSE
PINEAPPLE FRITTERS, KIRSCH SAUCE

LALLA ROOKH PUNCH
LEMON WAFERS

ROAST GOSLING, MARJORAM DRESSING, APPLE SAUCE

ROMAINE AND NASTURTIUM   LETTUCE AND TOMATO, MAYONNAISE

WHITE MOUNTAIN PUDDING, SHERRY SAUCE   BRANDY JELLY
LEMON MERINGUE PIE
CHERRY PIE   PHILADELPHIA ICE CREAM
TUTTI FRUTTI ICE CREAM IN FORM   DEL CORONADO CHOCOLATE CREAMS
FANCY ASSORTED CAKE   FARD DATES
SNOWFLAKES   WATER CRACKERS   CALIFORNIA FIGS
FRUITS   NUTS   RAISINS
ROQUEFORT, EDAM, SWISS, CALIFORNIA CAMEMBERT AND AMERICAN CHEESE
TEA   COFFEE

MEAL HOURS:	PROGRAMME.
Breakfast 6:30 to 10:00	1 MARCH—"Eleven O'clock Toast" .... *Winstein*
Sunday 7:30 to 10:00	2 OVERTURE—"Bohemian Girl" .... *Balfe*
Luncheon 12:30 to 2:00	3 CORNET SOLO—"The Holy City" .... *Adams*
Dinner 6:00 to 8:00	4 SELECTION—"Merry Wives of Windsor" .... *Nicolai*
Nurses and Children:	5 BALLET MUSIC from "Faust" .... *Art. by Mases-Tobani*
Breakfast 6:30 to 9:00	6 Military March No. 1 .... *Schubert*
Luncheon 12:00 to 1:30	
Dinner 5:30 to 7:30	HENRY OEHLMEYER, Director

NO SEATS RESERVED AFTER 6:30 O'CLOCK

SUNDAY, APRIL 7, 1901

Easter Day.

*The Hotel del Coronado's 1901 Easter
offerings included entertainment.*

Easter Candy

By the turn of the century, Easter candy had become a seasonal tradition. It began in a small way in the late 1800s with a few random newspaper ads, but by the early 1900s, store ads filled papers across the West with candy selections. The Helena, Montana, firm of Bach, Cory & Company noted they had many confections, including cocoa bonbons, cream pecans, crystal nougatines, jelly strawberries, cream filberts, dipped chocolates, Montana caramels, Boss peppermints, marshmallow bananas, Helena crystal fig sticks, jelly beans, and twenty other "toothsome" brands of candies from a leading Chicago confectioner. They noted that their candies and confections could be "all dumped in our Easter candy basket."

Sacramento merchants offered taffy and fruit and nut glacés, and the *Record-Union* placed a notice in their Easter edition about the candy at Welch Brothers. They wrote, "Lovers of the sweet and beautiful will be pleased at the efforts made by Welch Bros., the popular confectioners. Their store has been decorated in the most artistic fashion with palms and Easter lilies. Their stock of confectionery includes some of the rarest and choicest chocolates. Ice cream and delicious water ices are on hand in abundance to be served with the toothsome confections. The store is worth visiting if you don't spend a cent."

Egg Toss: Competitors toss their hard-boiled eggs in the air to see how many times it takes to crack their eggs. The one with the most tosses wins.

Egg Roll: Each person takes their egg and, one at a time, allows the eggs to roll down a board. The object is to strike the other eggs that have already been rolled down. The person who hits or scatters the most eggs is the winner.

Easter Bonnets

This little girl on the postcard looks properly dressed and all ready for Easter (ca. 1900s). SHERRY MONAHAN

Candy wasn't the only thing making a statement on the frontier. Fashionable dresses, hats, and clothing also became more prominent. The Sacramento firm of Weinstock, Lubin & Company took the opportunity to sell various items they noted were perfect for the Easter holiday. Under the heading of "Easter Millinery" they noted, "In trimmed hats for Easter we are showing all the latest ideas, including many choice copies of costly imported hats. In untrimmed straws we have beautiful shapes in all the different straws, including the new shades of olive and brown. In Children's and Misses' trimmed millinery we have many things suitable for Easter." They advertised Persian and Dresden ribbons and millinery flowers, which included rose sprays, cowslips, natural roses, and more. To add to the ladies' hat options, they offered ornaments of rhinestone, gilt, and pearl were available. For gifts, they advertised "beautiful Easter cards and booklets, mottled glass Easter eggs—some painted ones with gilt . . . real China egg cups, the upper part covered by half of a real egg shell, beneath which is concealed some amusing object." Fashionable Easter wear had become a social expectation.

Easter Recipes from the Frontier

These recipes and foods are suggested by the Victorian pioneers themselves. They include foods that use eggs, traditional dinners, and Easter-themed foods. Some tasty Easter dishes included leg of lamb and hot cross buns. The recipes are from newspapers all over the West to ensure this is what the pioneers were cooking.

The Hotel Spokane offered an elegant Easter menu in 1899. COURTESY OF THE NEW YORK PUBLIC LIBRARY

ESCALLOPED EGGS

SERVES 2-4

6 eggs, hard boiled

1¼ teaspoons cayenne pepper

½ teaspoon salt, or to taste

¼ teaspoon white pepper, or to taste

1 tablespoon milk

½ teaspoon onion powder

2 tablespoons bread crumbs

¼ cup butter

Peel and chop the eggs and place them in a bowl. Add the cayenne, salt, white pepper, milk, and onion powder. Stir to combine.

Place the mixture in a buttered baking dish, cover with the bread crumbs, and dot with butter. Bake in a 400°F oven for 20 to 30 minutes.

Adapted from the *Fort Worth Morning Register*, 1899

EGGS À LA PARISIENNE

SERVES 2–4

1½ cups cheddar cheese, grated

6 eggs

Salt and pepper to taste

¼ cup heavy cream

Liberally butter a baking dish and sprinkle half the cheese to cover the bottom. Gently break the eggs into the dish and season with salt and pepper. Add the cream and top with the remaining cheese. Bake at 350°F for about 20 minutes, or until the egg whites are set.

Recipe adapted from *El Dorado* (Kansas) *Daily Republican*, 1905

ROAST LEG OF LAMB WITH MINT SAUCE

SERVES 4-6

5 pounds bone-in lamb leg

3 tablespoons canola or olive oil

Salt and freshly ground black pepper

Mint Sauce (recipe follows)

Preheat the oven broiler to high. Allow the lamb to come to room temperature, which should take about 30 minutes.

Place the lamb in a roasting pan, coat it with the oil, and liberally season it with salt and pepper. Broil the lamb for about 5 minutes or until golden. Remove from the oven and turn it over. Broil the other side the same way.

Remove the lamb from the oven and preheat the oven to 325°F. Loosely cover the lamb with foil and cook for about 2 hours for a medium lamb, or until a meat thermometer registers 135°F. Remove the lamb from the oven and allow to rest for 20 minutes before serving. Slice the lamb and arrange it on a serving platter.

MINT SAUCE

MAKES 2 CUPS

2 cups vinegar

3 teaspoons sugar

2 bunches fresh mint, chopped

Bring the vinegar to a boil over medium-high heat in a saucepan. Add the sugar and stir to dissolve. Add the mint, stir, and allow to cool before serving with the lamb.

Recipes adapted from Omaha, Nebraska's *World Herald*, 1899

GREEN PEAS

SERVES 4

4 cups fresh or frozen peas

3 tablespoons butter

½ heavy cream

Salt and pepper to taste

If using fresh peas, cover with water and boil over medium-high heat for 20 minutes. If using frozen, cook according to package directions. Drain the peas and place them back in the warm saucepan. Melt the butter and then add the cream; salt and pepper to taste.

Recipe adapted from the *Topeka* (Kansas) *Daily Capital*, 1905

HOT CROSS BUNS

MAKES ABOUT 20 ROLLS

1 egg, beaten

1½ cups warm milk

1 ounce yeast

3½–4 cups flour

½ teaspoon allspice

¾ cup (1½ sticks) butter

¾ pound currants

1 cup confectioners' sugar

1 tablespoon milk

In a small bowl, combine the egg, milk, and yeast. Stir to blend and let sit to dissolve the yeast. Combine 3 cups of the flour and allspice together in a large bowl. Rub the butter and currants into the flour until crumbly. Create a well in the center of the flour and pour in the egg-yeast mixture. Mix together until a soft ball is formed. Gradually add the remaining flour if the dough is too wet. Knead on a lightly floured surface until the dough is smooth and springs back when touched.

Place in a greased bowl and slash a cross into the top. Dust with flour. Cover and allow to rise in a warm place until doubled in size. When the dough has risen, punch it down. Divide the dough into as many rolls as you want. Shape into balls and make a cross in the tops with a knife.

Place on greased baking sheets, about 4 inches apart. Bake at 375°F for about 20 minutes, or until golden brown. Combine confectioners' sugar and milk, and paint the crosses on the buns.

Recipe adapted from the *Los Angeles Times*, 1899

EASTER CAKE

MAKES 1 CAKE

3 cups granulated sugar

1 cup butter, softened

3 cups flour

2 teaspoons baking powder

1 cup milk

1 teaspoon lemon extract

6 egg whites

½ pound confectioners' sugar

¼ cup water

½ pound figs, chopped

½ pound golden raisins

½ pound crushed almonds

Combine the granulated sugar, butter, flour, baking powder, milk, and the lemon extract in a large mixer bowl. Beat on low speed for about 1 minute.

Scrape down and beat on high speed for 2 minutes, scraping the bowl occasionally.

Add the egg whites and beat an additional 2 minutes on high speed.

Grease and flour two cake pans or a tube pan and pour in the batter.

Bake at 350°F for 40 to 45 minutes, or until wooden pick inserted in center comes out clean.

Allow the cake to rest in the pans for 10 minutes and then cool on cake racks.

While the cake is baking, make the icing. Combine the confectioners' sugar and water in a mixing bowl. If it's too watery, add some more sugar. It needs to be thick enough to stick to the outside of the cake. Add the figs, raisins, and nuts and stir to combine. Spread the icing between the cake layers and cover the sides and top.

Decorate with colored candy eggs.

Recipe adapted from El Dorado, Kansas's *Walnut Valley Times*, 1891

CHAPTER FOUR

THE FOURTH OF JULY

KIMBALL WEBSTER, A TWENTY-ONE-YEAR-OLD NEW HAMPSHIRE farmer who headed west to California with the rush of gold miners in April 1849, wrote with awe about the celebrations at his mining camp on Independence Day 1849: "The Fourth of July will remind an American of his home wherever he may be or however far he may be separated from it. Early in the morning we fired several rounds, and made as much noise as possible in honor of the day of Independence. We started in the morning and soon passed an encampment where we had the pleasure of beholding the 'Star Spangled Banner' floating in the cool breeze."

When gold was discovered in California in 1849, America was just eighty-four years old, so celebrating its freedom anniversary was a big deal—as it still is. Some pioneers even had grandfathers who served in the Revolutionary War.

Fourth of July celebrations in the Old West, as well as the rest of America, followed the suggestions that patriot John Adams shared in a letter to his wife, Abigail, in the days after independence was declared. In 1864 Kansas's *Leavenworth Daily Conservative* reprinted his letter: "The Second Day of July 1776, will be the most memorable epoch, in the History of America. I am apt to believe that it will be celebrated, by succeeding Generations, as the great anniversary Festival. It ought to be commemorated, as the Day of Deliverance by solemn Acts of Devotion to God Almighty. It ought to be solemnized with Pomp and Parade, with Shews, Games, Sports, Guns, Bells, Bonfires and Illuminations from one End of this Continent to the other from this Time forward forever more."

Even though Adams thought July 2 was the most significant day to celebrate, the Fourth became our national holiday. Oddly enough, Adams died on July 4, fifty years after the signing of the Declaration of Independence, just hours after Thomas Jefferson died.

The best flag under the sun:
Under it, Liberty was won.

Celebrations across the country closely followed Adams's wishes. They were often kicked off with a parade or a cannon blast, which was then followed with a benediction by the local minister or priest. Orations by city officials and local business owners came next, and the reading of the Declaration of Independence was a featured highlight. Most businesses closed, people decorated with red, white, and blue, and they proudly displayed Old Glory. Festivities, including races, swimming competitions, baseball games, band music, and picnics, filled the day and the evening culminated with fireworks, which included, not unlike today, rockets, Roman candles, pigeons, squibs, tourbillions, and wheels. Pioneers also sent patriotic postcards to their loved ones when they couldn't be with them.

Festive postcard that was sent by pioneers (ca. 1900s). SHERRY MONAHAN

Regardless of where people lived on the frontier, they found a way to celebrate the Fourth of July. From quiet sips of lemonade under shady trees to elaborate meals and fireworks, the pioneers openly and patriotically celebrated the birth of their nation.

Independence Rock

Whether in towns or along the trails, pioneers took time to honor their country's independence. In 1852 William Henry Hart traveled along the Overland Trail and kept a detailed diary along the way. They had passed the notable landmark called Independence Rock in Wyoming on July 1. If the pioneers didn't make the rock by July 4, which is how the rock received its name, then they were likely to hit snow in the mountains as they continued their journey west.

Hart wrote about their Fourth of July celebration:

July 4th at daylight about a dozen of the early risers (myself not included) ushered in the day and rinsed out the lazy ones by a "few de joie" of double barrelled guns rifles & pistols and soon all were stirring about preparing breakfast and planning the days programme. Reed started out early for game and the ladies brought out a handsome flag composed of red, white, & blue stripes and patches taken from sundry garments supposed to form parts of female wearing apparel. A line had been rigged, out of various cords of various sizes in use about the train, and the Stars and Stripes floated in the breeze amidst the cheers and waving handkerchiefs of the entire party. Breakfast over we set to work to rig a tent awning for our table while some went after the pish and rails for it. We drove crutched sticks into the ground and laid the rails across from one to another and laid across them all the boards we could muster, our wagon decks answering the purpose very well. We then built an arbor over it and covd [covered] that with our awning. The wind rose and began to blow the dust and dry leaves & grass about so that we had to further protect our dining room by hanging over blankets all around it making the walls of the structure. We ornamented the whole concern as well as we could with the boughs cut from the pish and rails and with all the wild flowers we could gather. Reed returned with a horse load of Antelope and prairie fowl which were soon picked, dressed and in the hands of the cooks. At about 3 o.c. the (Tin pan) Gong sounded the call to dinner and we found there a fine set out of Antelope, roasted & stewed Prairie Fowl do & do. Smoked Beef do. Bacon fried & boiled. Dried apples & Peaches, Rice, Beans Bread & crackers with an ample supply of Tea & Coffee and Bean Soup. Of course all were in good spirits and enjoyed the feast as only emigrants over a weary road know how to. The table being cleared of its edibles the dishes were piled one side and the brandy brought out. All who wanted any (myself not included) passed up their glasses (which as well as all the plates & Dishes were of pure tin) and received their allowance. There was just enough to give each a good draw. The rest of us filled up with water and "The Day," the "President," the "Union." the "Ladies" &c&c were each toasted & cheered in all due formality, finally V. Y. Ralston was called on for a speech and bodily lifted upon the table. He gave us a short but very appropriate address displaying real talent and eloquence. Others were called on and forcibly put upon the table but after a few efforts the scene of boisterous merriment was ended by the table coming down with a grand crash but no serious damage. Then all hands were mustered for parade and went through a ludicrous imitation of the exercise. After which all joined in a grand game of ball (the ball was found amoung the children's play things) and at sunset a national salute of 100 guns (more or less) ended our fourth of July and as pleasant a one as ever I spent. After dark our camp soon became quiet and all sought early that rest that was to refresh us for our journey onwards.

Local Celebrations

Even though the Kansas Territory was struggling with the issue of slavery in the mid-1800s and many of the residents were caught in the middle, citizens took time to celebrate the nation's birthday. One resident was Sara C. Robinson and her husband Charles, who arrived in Kansas in 1854 as affiliates of the New England Emigrant Aid Company. They moved to Kansas to counter proslavery efforts and ensure that Kansas joined the Union as a free state. She had kept a journal of their efforts, and in 1856 she penned a book titled *Kansas: Its Interior and Exterior Life*. She often used a single letter for people's last names, so it's hard to know whom she was referring to in some cases. In her book she wrote of Independence Day:

> *The morning of the Fourth came in cloudy, yet pleasant. Word had been sent to the people on the Wakarusa, and many were expected. Invitations also were sent to the Delaware and Shawnee Indians to mingle in our festivities. From the elevated position of our house we saw the people gathering from all quarters. Several teams, of oxen as well as horses, the roughness of the vehicles being hidden under garlands of green leaves and flowers, came in from the Wakarusa. A beautiful flag was presented by a Massachusetts lady to the military companies of Lawrence, in an appropriate speech, in behalf of the ladies of Lawrence. After its acceptance, the procession formed upon Massachusetts street and was escorted by the military to a fine grove about a mile from town. Here, in one of Nature's grand old forests, seats had been provided, and a platform raised for the orators and other speakers, for the singers and musical instruments. The number present was variously estimated from fifteen hundred to two thousand. It was a motley gathering. There were many people with eastern dress and manner, and settlers from Missouri, and other far western states, no less distinctly marked by theirs. The Delawares and Shawnees added no little to the interest of the occasion. After the reading of the Declaration of Independence, whose embodied truths seemed to have gained new vitality,*

new force, since we last listened to it, came the oration. It was, for the most part, a gathering together of the opinions of southern men upon the vexed question of slavery. There were confessions as to the relative value of free and slave labor by some of their best educated men. There was a most perfect condemnation of the whole system from their own mouths. Then the question of our own position, in regard to the encroachments of a neighboring state, was touched upon, with the firm determination to assert our rights, and maintain them. There were speeches, songs, and sentiments. We received friendly words of welcome from the chiefs of the Delawares and Shawnees. They were glad to see us coming, not with the hatchet and sounds of war, but bringing with us the sweet fruits of peace and civilization. A long day was quickly passed—the first Fourth of July in Kansas celebrated by its white settlers. In the evening a party of about one hundred was gathered, to strengthen yet more the bonds of social feeling, in our largest hall, which serves the purpose of church, school-room, and hall for all political and social meetings. We had refreshments of cakes and ice-creams, and our house full, as usual, at night.*

In 1860 in San Francisco the local paper ran a full page of the day's activities. The *Daily Evening Bulletin* reported that "the Fourth of July—the 84th Anniversary of our National Independence—was celebrated yesterday with spirit, and creditably." The day began at 8:30 a.m. with a twenty-one-gun salute by the National Guard. It was followed with a parade and a formal ceremony, which included a prayer, the reading of the Declaration of Independence, and the band played "America" and the "Star Spangled Banner." A local poet named J. F. Bowman wrote and read a poem.

---

* See An Oration on the Subject of Independence sidebar.

AN ORATION ON THE SUBJECT OF INDEPENDENCE

THE FOLLOWING IS THE CONCLUSION OF AN ORATION by a "Dr. R." from Sara Robinson's recollection of the Kansas celebration of Independence Day from her book *Kansas: Its Interior and Exterior Life.*

Fellow-citizens, in conclusion, it is for us to choose for ourselves, and for those who shall come after us, what institutions shall bless or curse our beautiful Kansas. Shall we have freedom for all the people, and consequent prosperity, or slavery for a part, with the blight and mildew inseparable from it? Choose ye this day which you will serve, — Slavery or Freedom, — and then be true to your choice. If slavery is best for Kansas, then choose it; but, if liberty, then choose that.

Let every man stand in his place, and acquit himself like a man who knows his rights, and, knowing, dares maintain them. Let us repudiate all laws enacted by foreign legislative bodies, or dictated by Judge Lynch, over the way. Tyrants are tyrants, and tyranny is tyranny, whether under the garb of law, or in opposition to it. So thought, and so acted, our ancestors; and so let us think and act. We are not alone in this contest. The entire nation is agitated upon the question of our rights; the spirit of '76 is breathing upon some; the hand-writing upon the wall is being discerned by others; while the remainder the gods are evidently preparing for destruction. Every pulsation in Kansas vibrates to the remotest artery of the body politic; and I seem to hear the millions of freemen, and the millions of bondsmen, in our own land, the millions of the oppressed in other lands, the patriots and philanthropists of all countries, the spirits of the revolutionary heroes, and the voice of God, all saying to the people of Kansas, "Do your duty!"

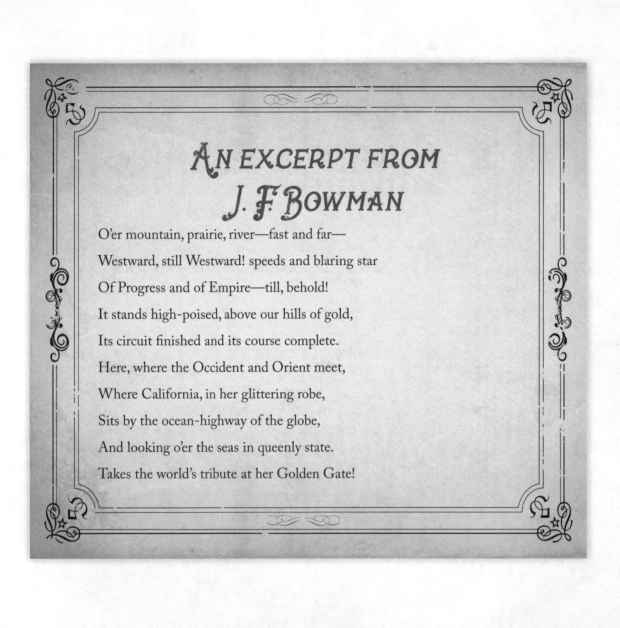

An Excerpt from
J. F. Bowman

O'er mountain, prairie, river—fast and far—

Westward, still Westward! speeds and blaring star

Of Progress and of Empire—till, behold!

It stands high-poised, above our hills of gold,

Its circuit finished and its course complete.

Here, where the Occident and Orient meet,

Where California, in her glittering robe,

Sits by the ocean-highway of the globe,

And looking o'er the seas in queenly state.

Takes the world's tribute at her Golden Gate!

Later that evening the city provided fireworks. The paper reported that

the North Beach end of town was all "on a crawl" long before sunset . . . at 8 ¼ o'clock
the pyrotechnic display commenced, and was maintained brilliant for over an hour.
First came a display of Bengal lights, shells, and rockets. . . . The set pieces were a Saxon,

This view is from
Austin's Building on
Montgomery Street
during the Fourth of July
parade in San Francisco,
July 1865. COURTESY OF
THE NEW YORK PUBLIC
LIBRARY

a Maltese cross, a maelstrom, a pyramid of candies, a "full glory," a vortex, a palm tree,
a double palm, a temple of the sun, Bunker Hill, and in conclusion, the Eagle of '76. . . .
Within a circuit of two rods on Greenwich street, more than a dozen fell before 9
o'clock—why they did not spoil somebody's skull-cap, is a miracle of mercy.

While San Francisco's paper dedicated an entire page to their celebration Austin, Texas's *State Gazette* that same year buried the tiny story at the bottom of page two. They reported, "The day passed off quietly. The Germans gave a festival at a little distance from town. There was also an oration and the reading of the Declaration of Independence at the Methodist Church, and at night Buass [assembly hall] gave a ball. A picnic at Manchaca took off many citizens who desired a little change from town to country life."

Miss Nettie Spencer, who grew up in Oregon in the late 1870s, proved how big an event the Fourth of July celebration was in her town by the amount of pies her mother made: "The big event of the year was the Fourth of July. Everyone in the countryside got together on that day for the only time in the year. Everyone would load their wagons with all the food they could haul and come to town early in the morning. On our first big Fourth at Corvallis mother made two hundred gooseberry pies. You can see what an event it was."

Englishman Henry Hilsop arrived in Los Angeles, California, on his way to Tucson, Arizona, to experience the one-hundredth anniversary of America's independence. He noted that on July 3 pioneers "let off" fireworks and were shooting off anvils until midnight. He wrote home to his grandmother back in England and described the Fourth of July proceedings:

At about 10 a.m. a grand procession was paraded through the streets to celebrate
Independence Day and this year being the centennial of course there was a grander
procession than usual. The first part was very tame but soon the scene enlivened by the

Los Angeles celebrated the Fourth of July in grand style in 1876. COURTESY OF THE UNIVERSITY OF SOUTHERN CALIFORNIA LIBRARY AND THE CALIFORNIA HISTORICAL SOCIETY

appearance of the fire-brigade and their red and blue jerseys. The engines were drawn by 6 horses, each pair having a suit of clothing red, white and blue calico and the engines all decorated with flowers. Then came the fire-escapes and hose-carts drawn by about 30 men each. They never use horses to the last mentioned. After these came a lot of girls in wagons dressed like fairies to represent different states and then came advertisements of people in business in the two such as upholsterers who paraded a suite of furniture on a wagon laid out like a drawing-room, then coopers who were making tubs and hogsheads as they were drawn on very large wagons along the streets, blacksmiths in the same manner as last but not least a party of miners, emigrants, and Indians as you see them traveling through the country, going through all kinds of antics. In the evening, there was a fire, so away I rushed as I was at the time in my bedroom. The engines were very soon on the spot and then came the hose and fire-escapes drawn by a number of men, the mob all helping. You always know when there is a fire as the bells being to ring. They soon put it out and then went to finish the 4th of July in the drinking saloons.

Skagway, Alaska, was one of the last frontier towns in the West. Scores of hopeful pioneers headed to the Klondike in search of gold. Even in the farthest reaches of the American West, the pioneers found a way to celebrate the Fourth of July in 1898. As far away as San Francisco, people heard of the celebration and, according to the *San Francisco Chronicle*, Skagway's celebration was the greatest event in the city's history. Even the governor made an appearance. In 1899 the town planned a grand celebration that included an afternoon parade, followed by games. The parade included the US band, the National Guard, city officials, school children, floats of secret societies, floats of businessmen, the local band, fire department, and a "pioneer" section that included miners and packers. In the evening, they listened to speeches and enjoyed fireworks over the Alaskan sky. In 1904 Skagway planned a celebration with many competitions and games. Hurdling, running, broad jumping, shot putting, hammer throwing, and baseball games between Whitehorse, Juneau, and Skagway were some of them. There were also bicycle races, pole vaults, pie-eating contests, tennis, shooting, boxing, and tug-of-war rounding out the games. The evening ended with a much-anticipated fireworks display.

As the West was becoming more refined and populated, small towns like Sheffield, Iowa; Mayville, North Dakota; and Sauk Centre, Minnesota, had parades and big Fourth of July celebrations. While Sheffield held a parade, the town of Sauk Centre offered its residents a baseball game. On July 4, 1908, residents visited the baseball field and track to watch their team play. They walked, rode horses, and drove their horse and buggies. Some enjoyed the game from the comfort of their shaded rides, while other sat in the stands.

A tug-of-war contest on the street in Skagway, Alaska, on the Fourth of July shows participants and a large group of spectators (ca. 1900s). COURTESY OF THE LIBRARY OF CONGRESS

A view of a street in Skagway, Alaska, on the Fourth of July (ca. 1900s). A group of spectators awaits the parade. COURTESY OF THE LIBRARY OF CONGRESS

1908 Independence Day parade in Sheffield, Iowa COURTESY OF THE LIBRARY OF CONGRESS

Fourth of July parade, Mayville, North Dakota, 1908 COURTESY OF THE LIBRARY OF CONGRESS

A 1908 baseball game within a race track on the prairie, horse and buggies surround the track. The stands and church can also be seen.
COURTESY OF THE LIBRARY OF CONGRESS

Baseball, Parades, and Races

In addition to parades and fireworks, baseball was a big event for many Fourth of July celebrations, but most were local teams competing against one another. Professional teams had played in the National League since 1876, which just happened to be the year that America was celebrating her one-hundredth anniversary of independence. That year, the only team on the frontier was the St. Louis Brown Stockings, and they played the Boston Red Caps on July 4 that year. They lost 3–4. The following year they played the Hartford Dark Blues on July 4 and won 7–6. Some of their players had colorful names, including Joe Battin, Davy Force, and Tricky Nichols.

1—Boyle. 5—Chamberlain. 9—Browns Mascot. 13—Milligan.
2—White. 6—Robinson. 10—McCarthy. 14—King.
3—Hudson. 7—Latham. 11—O'Neill. 15—Nolan.
4—Devlin. 8—Capt. Comiskey. 12—Lyons. 16—Hey

The Famous World Beaters
ST. LOUIS BROWNS.
Champions of Am. Association Four Successive Years, 1885, '86, '87, '88.
Worlds Champions, 1886, 1887.

Playing baseball in July was as popular in the 1800s as it is today. Here the St. Louis Browns play a game in 1888.
COURTESY OF THE LIBRARY OF CONGRESS

After the parades and speeches, pioneers enjoyed horse races, pedestrian races, boat races, shooting competitions, and picnics. Some places, like Wyoming in 1867, had a friendly game of baseball with the local boys and men, while some towns and cities had their own teams and played other nearby "rival" teams in matches. In the 1870s San Francisco had their Athletic Baseball Club, Denver's team was also called the Athletics, and Little Rock, Arkansas, had the Giants.

Baseball was also played on the Fourth of July in Tombstone, Arizona. This silver-mining town was very proud of their local team, which was often referred to as the Picked Nine. The entire town displayed their patriotism. Store owners in the 1880s braved ladders to drape red, white, and blue patriotic bunting from their buildings, while others simply sported Old Glory. In 1886 the Comet Saloon erected a shade platform for those wanting to dance outside, where it was cooler. There were horse races at Doling's track, and the Elite Theatre (aka Bird Cage) provided a beautiful patriotic display of fireworks in front of the theater. Before the fireworks, a hot-air balloon ascended into the high desert's blue sky. Tombstone's in-ground swimming pool was also reopened on the Fourth with great fanfare. Not only did they offer new bathing suits for rental, but they opened a first-class bar at the bathhouse. Tombstone's fire department, as well as other organizations, mulled over whether or not they should have a parade that year.

Deadwood in the Dakota Territory had no problem in deciding on a parade or not in 1888. They had a grand one that began at ten o'clock. By 9:00 a.m., the main street was thronged with eager parade watchers. Men, women, and children replete in their Victorian clothing stood about, joking, laughing, talking, and shouting as they waited. The peaceful but excited crowd began to cheer as the procession began. Marshal Knight of the cornet band took the lead and was followed by the Deadwood Pioneer Hook and Ladder Company, the Homestake Hose Company, the South Deadwood Hose Company, the Chinese running team, and the Chinese band wagon team. They were all followed by various carriages in which the mayor and other prominent citizens were carried. After the parade, as many as could fit filled the opera house for orations, songs, and prayers.

Next up was the fire hose tournament called the "hub and hub" that commenced at 3:00 p.m. The competitors included a team called the Independents of Council Bluffs, Iowa, and Deadwood's own team, called the Deadwoods. These two teams were the only two Chinese hose companies in the country at the time. The *Aberdeen Daily News* reported, "Smashed the Firemen's Record. In the 300 yards hub-and-hub hose race yesterday afternoon for a $500 prize, between the Independents of Council Bluffs, Iowa, and Deadwoods of Deadwood, the latter won by four feet in twenty-nine seconds, which beats the world's record [by] one second." Within fifteen minutes from the time victorious Deadwood crossed the line, satin badges bearing the printed words *Deadwood Hose, World's Champions* were pinned to the shirts of each member of the team. The day's events ended as many did, with a pyrotechnic display, which took place on the East hill. People tilted their heads upward to revel in a colorful spectrum. They gazed at Roman candles, rockets, shower of gold and silver light, and a rainbow of waterfalls and other patriotic pieces.

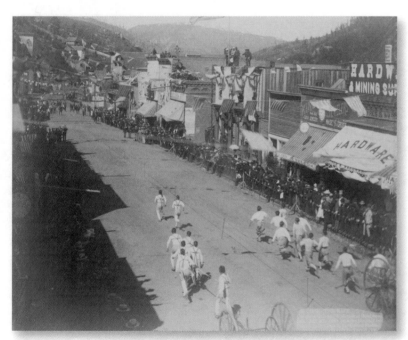

The great hub-and-hub hose race in Deadwood, Dakota Territory, on July 4, 1888. Two small teams of Chinese runners pulled a hose and wagon, racing down main street with a large crowd of spectators on both sides of street. COURTESY OF THE LIBRARY OF CONGRESS

Loomis, Iowa, paid special attention to the late afternoon events during their 1894 Fourth of July celebration that included multiple activities. They began the day with all the traditional events, like orations, a parade, and an afternoon barbecue. From 2:30 to 5:30 p.m., pioneers could watch competitive horse races of various times and distances. If horse racing didn't hold their interest, then they could head to the baseball field between 3:00 and 6:00 p.m. to watch the baseball game. Loomis's team was playing against the "picked nine from the country." The winners received a baseball and bat. From 4:00 to 6:00 p.m., general amusements included rope walking and several races—sack, three-legged, greased pig, goose baiting, wheelbarrow, free for all foot, potato, rooster pulling, and egg. There was also a tug-of-war between ten men on each side, with the winning team earning a box of cigars. Later that evening the town promised over three hundred pieces of fireworks of superior quality that was "the grandest display of fireworks ever witnessed in Phelps County."

Another competition in Steamboat Springs, Colorado, in 1904 became a little more serious. As was typical in many locales, they celebrated the Fourth with a baseball game, but a little more than pride and bragging rights were on the line. Editors of their local papers chose the teams who would compete and bet each other their team would be victorious. Charles H. Leckenby was the *Pilot*'s editor, and John Weiskopf was the *Sentinel*'s. The editors decided that the loser of the bet would have to shave off his moustache. There was more to the bet, which the *Denver Post* reported:

> *The loser to shave off his moustache and refrain from treating or being treated for a period of three months, and turn his paper over to the local Ladies' W.C.T.U. [Women's Christian Temperance Union] for one week, in all matters following the copy they shall send in. The Sentinels won by a score of 13 to 10. The crowd which witnessed the game was the largest ever gathered on the Steamboat diamond. Under written agreement the losing editor is to carry out his wager under penalty of forfeiting a $25 suit of clothes*

and announce his intention of fulfilling the bet. The teams were chosen from among the local players and was hotly contested.

Picnics and Banquets

While many towns across the frontier knew exactly how to celebrate the Fourth, in 1889 the editor of St. Louis's *Republic* asked for citizens' input and suggestions on the best way to celebrate America's independence. Resident William Hyde wrote, "First—Perhaps the best way is for him to take his family to some cool spot in the country where there is a sufficient 'contiguity of shade' and a stream of clear water. Let him also take a very big chunk of ice, some still Catawba, lemons, and powdered sugar, together with soft white bread, caviar or deviled ham, broiled chicken (spring, but not Timken spring), Jersey butter, and such cake and confectionery as will please the part of the other part."

While recipes for deviled or potted ham were made at home by pioneers, they easily could have purchased a common brand still used today. In fact, many pioneers carried cans of deviled ham in their wagons when they went west. William Underwood began his business in the early 1800s, and in 1868 they created deviled ham in a can. Two years later they were granted a patent for their current world-famous logo—the little red devil. Ads depicting the little red devil began to appear nationally as early as 1895. Today, the Underwood devil is one of the oldest existing trademarks still in use in the United States. Because not all pioneer women had access to the canned version, women like Nellie B. Ward submitted this hint and recipe to Sacramento's *Record-Union* in 1890, "If potted ham is not conveniently near, you can prepare a most excellent filling by mincing ham very fine and seasoning with pepper, mustard and celery salt, rub all together and add a little butter to make it a thick paste. Put the sandwiches in a basket with low sides."

While picnics were a popular way to celebration the nation's birth, restaurants in bigger cities tended to offer special, and sometimes patriotic, menus. In 1892 the Saddle Rock restaurant in Salt Lake City, Utah, offered a fine Fourth of July menu, and the bill of fare included chicken, duck, turkey, roast beef, strawberry shortcake, and of course, ice cream. French fried potatoes became a popular menu item by the late 1800s and were served in restaurants and at picnics and celebrations.

A few years later the *Salt Lake Herald* reported that their town's 1898 Fourth of July celebration "was one of the biggest of the many big things that prime favorite of resorts has ever had. . . . Every department down to the popcorn venders did an enormous trade." Many western towns promoted their celebration by placing details of the day in their local papers. It was fairly common to see mention of a peanut and popcorn vendor in the list of attractions. One such company was the Sweet Candy Company. Leon Sweet began his business in Portland, Oregon, in 1892 but moved to Salt Lake City by the turn of the century. He donated candy and popcorn for the celebration in Portland in 1896.

What you ate depended on where you lived and what you could get your hands on. One thing that most people enjoyed was ice cream. Ice cream wasn't served in cones just yet, so ice cream plates and forks were used. It's also interesting to think about how ice cream was made on the frontier. First, ice had to be imported in large chunks and hacked away into usable pieces. Then the cream mixture had to be made and poured into the freezing vessel. The ice cream vessel was then placed in the churner, and ice and coarse salt were added. The last step was for someone to churn the machine by hand until the right consistency was achieved. After that, the ice cream could be served. The *Moberly Weekly Monitor* in Missouri wrote about their 1899 celebration: "By 8 o'clock the park was crowded, and while the Bachelors band played sweetly, the crowd watched the fireworks, ate ice cream and had a good time all around."

While Leavenworth, Kansas, didn't list their attractions for their celebration in the late 1890s, they did offer some whimsical poems in their June 30 paper.

The Fourth of July is almost here,

The day that America holds so dear;

The day of flags and cannon and bells,

When patriotism in each breast swells;

The day of fireworks gorgeous to view;

The day of burn fingers, and faces, too!

Oh, Fourth of July is almost here,

And we're thankful it comes but one a year!

Leavenworth Herald, June 30, 1894

"What does it mean to the one little maid?

Popcorn and peanuts and pink lemonade.

What does it mean to two little boys?

Torpedoes and fire-cracker, racket, and noise."

THE BELLS OF LIBERTY

Ring out, O bells of liberty!

Ring out with joys of mirth,

And send the rapture of your chimes

Around the listening earth;

Ring loud and clear that all may hear—

The fettered and the free—

Ring out, O bells! Ring once again,

A purer, holier chime,

And the echoes of your strain

Far up the hills of time;

Ring, ring, with clear prophetic voice

The bliss that yet shall be—

Say to earth, "Rejoice, rejoice!"

For love is liberty!

Ring, tunefull bells, ring sweet and clear

A hymn of prayer and praise

That God will guide us year by year

Through His appointed ways.

Ring, ring harmonious to his to His will,—

For only those are free

Who in the love of God fulfill

His law of liberty.

—Ida Whipple Benham

Leavenworth Herald, June 30, 1894

In addition to the ice cream vendors, the soda man did a good business during these celebrations. Ginger beer, also called pop or ale, was quite popular in the Victorian West and originated in England a century before the West was populated. Back in the day it was an alcoholic spirit served in saloons. It started to fall out of favor in America as the turn of the century neared and concerned citizens forced the Prohibition issue. It was replaced with a nonalcoholic version of ginger ale. The "beer" was sold at Fourth of July celebrations, bakeries, and saloons all over the West.

Cooking meat over an open pit was a mainstay of most picnics and celebrations. Pioneer men removed their jackets or vests and covered their boiled and starched shirts with aprons to begin the barbecue process. During the nineteenth century, and across the frontier, the term *barbecue* simply meant roasting meat over hot coals. Early in the day the men would gather at the designated barbecue spot, season the meat with salt and pepper, and roast it over hot coals in the open air. Once the meat was cooked, it was sliced and served between two pieces of bread.

While the men cooked over the hot, open flames, the Victorian ladies wore hats and held parasols to shade them from the heat as they enjoyed the picnics, barbecues, and French suppers across the West. Smaller towns like Carroll, Iowa, had more laidback events in 1900. The *Cedar Rapids Evening Gazette* reported that "Carroll citizens are people of quiet tastes and will spend the Fourth of July at home, reading the Declaration of

Independence, drinking lemonade in the shade, and helping the youngsters with their fireworks in the evening."

A tall, dark, and genteel Mrs. Hortense Watkins remembered how special the Fourth of July was on the frontier for her.

When I first came to [Eugene] Oregon we seemed to have just two big holidays, Christmas and Fourth of July. I believe there was more excitement at our house on the Fourth than at Christmas, because one and sometimes two of my daughters rode on the liberty car, and there was uproar for days before. Liberty cars [wagons] are something we don't hear anything of nowadays, but they were mighty pretty. And instead of queens and princesses as they have for everything today, there was Columbia. She sat up on top of the liberty car, and all the little States were grouped in tiers about her, each little girl in white, with a big sash down over her shoulder, showing the name of the State she represented. Columbia always had to have fair or golden hair. It didn't matter so much about the States, only they had to be pretty. The car was a big dray, all painted and draped with bunting and decorated with flowers and greens, with the seats arranged in rows one above the other. The car was drawn by four white horses, with lots of tassels and netting to set them off. The liberty car was the most important part of the parade, but the "plug uglies"—young blades about town all rigged out in masks and fantastic costumes—excited a lot of interest. Everybody guessing who they were. Once in a while they would get a little hoodlumish. I think that is why they were eventually ruled out. Anyway we mothers were always rather relieved when the parade was over and our little States returned safely to us. There was always the fear of a runaway, what with the firecrackers and everything to scare a horse. We usually had some dignitary from elsewhere to deliver the oration, and at night everybody turned out to see the fireworks—Roman candles and set pieces like the flag, George Washington, etc. Those were great days all right. I think everybody was happier then.

About sixty miles north of Eugene, Oregon, stood the town of Albany, which sits on the bank of the Willamette River, so swimming was a common event throughout the summer months. On one Fourth of July the town offered a funny swimming contest. The *Albany Democrat* reported, "One of the contests of the 4th of July will be a very laughable swimming match between eight or ten men. They will start in tights and swim to a raft, where they will put on stove pipe hats, swim back, and put on their pants, cross again and put on their coats, then again and get an umbrella which they will raise and swim back with, the man getting out first with the umbrella being the winner. It will afford an immense sight of sport."

Even though she didn't mention swimming, a petite, blue-eyed Mrs. Minnie Ford recalled her Fourth of July celebrations in Canyon City, Oregon:

> The Fourth of July celebrations were the great events in our lives. A typical celebration would be a picnic at noon, with barbecued sheep, hogs, and young steers. The tables would be piled high with the good food prepared by excellent cooks. After the picnic, everyone would gather around a platform that was set up in the middle of the grounds. The band would play patriotic pieces, and popular music of the day. A preacher would usually open the services with a long, dry, exhortation to God to preserve and protect the union. Judge Dustin, a noted character, of the day gave the Fourth of July speech. Always he read the Declaration of Independence. Then, he would deliver an excellent address. Mrs. Sagadoll, of whom I have spoken of, usually recited a patriotic piece of some kind. I have often heard told an amusing incident that occurred several years before my time. The Hon. J. C. Luce, arose to read the Declaration of Independence, his voice boomed out in clear, rich tones nearly half of the Constitution of the United States, before, H. W. Lair Hill pulled the tail of John's coat and informed him of his mistake. The evening of the Fourth was always spent in dancing. We would dance the Virginia Reel, Polkas, Schottische, Fireman's Dance, Mazurka, and the Varsovienne. At first

these dances were danced to the hop craze. We would hop, polka, and schottische. Later the glide craze came in and we would waltz to the Minuet and other glide dances.

Far from a quiet celebration, Juneau, Alaska, provided one of the most organized and entertaining Fourth of July celebrations in 1902. It started with a typical parade, which was followed by music at the opera house, and the reading of the Declaration. Songs included the "Star Spangled Banner," "Red, White, and Blue," and "America." At 1:00 p.m., the contests began with the boys and girls under-twelve races, a race for "old men," and one for Indians only. Cash prizes were awarded to all the winners. Next was barrel rolling, pole vaulting, running high jumping, standing broad jumping, climbing a greased pole, and a one-hundred-yard dash. On Front Street people could see Professor G. LeFraze walk a tightrope and perform on a trapeze. There were also an obstacle race, egg and spoon races, a pie-eating contest, and a mush-eating content. Cash prizes were also awarded for these competitions. For those with tenacity there was a drilling competition where contestants had to drill for fifteen minutes. This one required a $2.50 entry fee, but the prize was $100.00. There was only one requirement for all the competitions, and that was there had to be at least three people competing. A prize was awarded to the best decorated building in town, and special prizes were awarded for parade participants, including best decorated vehicle, most original and best-suited character, most comically dressed child, best appearing organized body of men marching, and largest organization in parade. One other prize was given to the lady presenting the most handsome badges to be worn by officers of the day. The badge had to be made of red, white, and blue, with gold or silver fringe, and had to be either round or oblong.

Festive Foods

By the turn of the century, chicken—specifically fried chicken—had been declared as necessary to the Fourth of July as turkey was to Thanksgiving—at least by the *Kansas City Star*. In 1903 they reported,

Fried Chicken is the Dish. Custom demands that it be eaten on the Fourth of July. . . . Just as roast turkey is the proper dish for Thanksgiving and spring lamb the piece de resistance for the Easter dinner, fried chicken has become the typical hunger defender on the Fourth of July. This has become all the more true, doubtless since the Fourth has come to be recognized as the opening of the picnic season. Whoever heard of a picnic without fried chicken? . . . Few people have a big dinner on the Fourth of July. It is the season for delicatessen and luncheon foods of all kinds. Whether a family goes picnicking or stays at home lighter meats and fresh fruits and green vegetables are satisfying to the normal appetite in this hot weather.

Not everyone wanted a hot dish to eat in the July heat, so the *Star* recommended "cool" dishes that included boiled ham that cost thirty to forty cents per pound, boiled tongue at forty to fifty cents, mortadella luncheon ham sausage, larded with nuts for twenty cents, smoked pork tenderloin at thirty-five cents, and bratwurst, liverwurst, wienerwurst, kosher and mettwurst, and salami. To accompany the meat, they suggested potato and chicken salad, along with pickles and new olives that were stuffed with anchovies, celery, and pimiento. They also suggested peanut butter sandwiches as well as chicken croquettes, and a variety of cheeses including cream, Roquefort, brick, and pineapple. For fresh fruits, they suggested strawberries, watermelons, peaches, plums, apricots, bananas, oranges, and tangerines.

Cheeses and fruits were a popular menu item for picnics, but also at restaurants. The Hotel Colorado served a lavish Fourth of July spread in 1900, despite the town quietly

The Hotel Colorado created a patriotic Fourth of July menu for its Glenwood Springs residents in 1900. Items included chicken broth à la Washington, consommé Lafayette, spring chicken à la Walter Raleigh, American fruit pudding, and Benedictine jelly. COURTESY OF THE NEW YORK PUBLIC LIBRARY

celebrating the day. The Hotel Colorado opened in 1893 and advertised they were "one of the finest hotels in America." They advertised three hundred rooms and one hundred private bathrooms. The hotel's location also allowed guests to enjoy the natural hot springs nearby.

The *Glenwood Post* reported, "The Fourth was celebrated in a quiet way at the Hotel Colorado by a special patriotic dinner menu, neatly printed on a folder containing the musical program of the orchestra for the evening, and by a hop at which Chester Keite and Will Allen assisted with a cake walk, which was gracefully done. Fireworks completed the day's festivities. While the day was not boisterously celebrated, it is probable that the guests enjoyed the day more than had there been a big crowd and a grand celebration."

In another section, they noted, "Glenwood was remarkably quiet on the Fourth as a great many of our inhabitants took advantage of the low railroad rates to visit neighboring points where patriotic programmes were in order. Over 200 of our citizens went up to Leadville while not a few visited friends in Aspen, Carbondale, and Rifle. However, the small boy and the noisy cracker were considerably in evidence and the few who remained in town were very forcibly reminded of the existence of the great holiday."

Fourth of July Recipes

Food played a big role in celebrating the birth of the nation. Served at events from picnics to church socials, these recipes include some popular pioneer celebratory dishes. These recipes and food are suggested by the Victorian pioneers themselves. They include foods that were portable for picnics and were refreshing for the summer heat. Some Fourth of July dishes included lemonade, barbecued beef, and fried chicken. The recipes are from newspapers all over the West.

Family and friends having a picnic to celebrate Independence Day in Colorado Springs, Colorado. Sherry Monahan's great-aunt Ivah Turner-Elliott and her family are pictured (ca. 1900s). SHERRY MONAHAN

GINGER BEER

MAKES ABOUT 10 CUPS

9 cups water

1 tablespoon fresh ginger, sliced

1 cup sugar

2 fresh lemon slices

½ teaspoon cream of tartar

¾ teaspoon fast-acting yeast

Place 3 cups of water, the ginger, sugar, lemon, and cream of tartar in a large stockpot and bring to a boil over high heat. Reduce the heat and let it simmer for 5 minutes. Add the remaining 6 cups of cold water and sprinkle the yeast over the top. Stir. Cover the pan with a lid and place it in a cool place overnight.

The next day, sterilize enough plastic bottles to hold the liquid, in hot, soapy water. Rinse and set them aside. It's important to use plastic bottles, since the fermenting can build up pressure and explode glass ones. Filter the liquid through a sieve into each bottle. Leave 3 inches at the top empty, to allow for gas buildup. Attach the lids tightly and leave the bottles in a cool place. Check every few hours, unscrewing the cap a little each time as the pressure builds up to allow the gases to escape. Refrigerate and continue to open the bottle daily for pressure release.

It's ready to drink when it's fizzy, which will be within 12 to 36 hours, depending on the temperature.

Recipe adapted from the *Iowa Daily State Register*, 1866

LEMONADE

SERVES 4–6

2 cups sugar

2 cups water

6 large lemons

1½ cups sparkling or tap water

Ice

Make a sugar syrup by combining the sugar and water in a saucepan and setting it over medium heat. Once the sugar has dissolved, remove the pan from the heat.

Roll the lemons on the counter to soften them. Peel the rind of 5 lemons, being careful not to include any of the bitter white pith. Drop the rinds into the sugar and allow them to steep for an hour or more.

Juice the 5 peeled lemons through a strainer to catch the seeds. Remove the peels from the sugar syrup and discard. Add the lemon juice into the sugar syrup and stir to blend. Take the remaining lemon and slice into rounds. Add the sparkling water.

Pour the lemonade into a pitcher and add the lemon slices. Serve over ice.

Twenty-one firemen pose on a hook-and-ladder truck, holding flowers, with mountains in the background (1912). COURTESY OF THE LIBRARY OF CONGRESS

Recipe adapted from the *Kansas City* (Missouri) *Times*, 1894

BARBECUED BEEF

SERVES 6–8

3 pounds 2-inch-thick beef, such as London broil

Barbecue Dressing

If using coals, let them get hot and white. If using a gas grill, heat to high.

Baste the meat with the dressing and then place on the grill. Sear, uncovered, for 2 to 4 minutes on one side for medium-rare. Do not press or move the meat.

After reaching the desired cooking time, flip the steak, baste with dressing, and grill for another 2 to 4 minutes, uncovered. Baste again, move to a cooler part of the grill, and cover. Turn and baste occasionally for about 30 minutes.

Allow to rest 5 to 10 minutes before slicing so the juices will be retained.

BARBECUE DRESSING

MAKES ABOUT 3 CUPS

2 cups cider vinegar

2 cups canned tomatoes, chopped

2 teaspoons red pepper flakes

1 teaspoon freshly ground black pepper

1 teaspoon salt

2 tablespoons butter

Simmer all the ingredients together until blended. The dressing can be stored in the refrigerator for up to 1 week.

Recipes adapted from *Camping and Camp Cooking*, 1909

FRIED CHICKEN

SERVES 4-6

3-pound chicken, cut up

Salt

1½ cups flour

½ teaspoon freshly ground pepper

2 eggs

2 cups bread crumbs

Lard or butter, enough to cover the chicken for frying

Place the chicken in a bowl, cover with water, and add 2 tablespoons salt. Soak for 2 hours. Drain and pat completely dry.

Place the flour, pepper, and 1 teaspoon salt in a shallow bowl.

Beat the eggs in a small bowl and place the bread crumbs in a bag or deep bowl.

Coat each piece of chicken with the flour, then dip each in the egg and then in the bread crumbs.

Heat the lard or butter in a large frying pan or dutch oven (cast iron is best) over medium-high heat.

Gently place the chicken in the hot oil, using tongs. The oil should bubble immediately after adding the chicken. Slowly add the chicken so the temperature does not drop, and work in batches to avoid overcrowding.

Fry the chicken until golden brown, turning once, 10 to 20 minutes, depending on the size of the pieces.

Check for doneness by piercing the meat; the juices should run clear. When done, place the chicken on paper towels or a wire rack to drain. Salt to taste.

Place the cooked chicken in a 180°F oven to keep warm while the other pieces are being cooked.

Note: Do not get water anywhere near the hot oil because it will cause the oil to explode.

Recipe adapted from Omaha, Nebraska's *World Herald*, 1899

CHICKEN CROQUETTES

SERVES 4

1¾ cups chicken, cooked and minced

1 teaspoon parsley, chopped

½ teaspoon salt

¼ teaspoon celery salt

¼ teaspoon freshly ground pepper

1 teaspoon lemon juice

¼ teaspoon minced onion

1 cup White Sauce (page 157)

Dry bread crumbs, for coating

3 eggs, beaten

Oil, for frying

Mix the first seven ingredients together in a bowl and stir well. Add enough of the white sauce to moisten the mixture, but do not allow it to become too soft. Form the mixture into your desired shapes, such as cones, balls, cylinders, and so on. Roll the shapes in the bread crumbs first, then in the beaten eggs, and then back in the bread crumbs.

Bring oil to a medium-high heat in a deep stockpot. Gently place the croquettes in the hot oil and cook until they are golden brown. Drain on paper towels and sprinkle with a little salt.

Note: This recipe would also work well with leftover turkey.

Recipe adapted from the *Sunday Oregonian*, 1902

DEVILED HAM

SERVES 4

2 cups lean boiled ham, chopped into pieces

¼ teaspoon freshly ground pepper

1 teaspoon celery salt

1 teaspoon mustard

1–3 teaspoons butter, melted

Grind the ham with a mortar and pestle into a paste. Place in a bowl or feel free to use a food processor to get a super-smooth consistency. Add the pepper, celery salt, mustard, and 1 teaspoon butter. Blend and add additional butter for the desired consistency. If it becomes too soupy, add a teaspoon of flour to thicken.

Spread on buttered bread and cut into sandwiches.

Festive postcards like these were sent and received by many pioneers (ca. 1900s). SHERRY MONAHAN

Recipe adapted from the *Sacramento Sunday Union,* September 14, 1890

POTATO SALAD

SERVES 8–10

5 pounds new potatoes

3 slices bacon, diced

1 onion, peeled and diced

½ cup white vinegar

¼ cup water

3–5 tablespoons flour

Salt and pepper to taste

Boil the unpeeled potatoes over high heat in a large pot until tender. The skins can be either removed or left on. Drain and set aside.

Fry the bacon in a skillet over medium heat until crispy. Remove the bacon but leave the grease in the pan. Set bacon aside.

Add the onion to the bacon grease along with the vinegar and water. Allow to boil over medium-high heat until the onion is soft. Mix 3 tablespoons flour with a small amount of water to make a paste. Add this to the boiling liquid and cook until thick. If it doesn't thicken, add more flour. Remove from the heat and allow to cool.

Once the mixture is cool, pour it over the potatoes. Gently toss and taste for seasoning.

Recipe adapted from the *Wichita* (Kansas) *Searchlight*, 1908

FRENCH FRIED POTATOES

SERVES 2-4

4 white or yellow potatoes

Oil, for frying

Salt

Cut the potatoes into pieces about 1 inch square and soak them in water overnight. The next morning, drain and dry them thoroughly. Any amount of water will cause the oil to pop and explode.

Add enough oil to a large stockpot to come up halfway and set it over medium-high heat. When hot, gently place the potatoes into the oil and cook them until lightly golden. Drain on paper towels and immediately sprinkle with salt.

Recipe adapted from the *Minneapolis Journal*, 1895

STRAWBERRY SHORTCAKE

SERVES 4

5½ cups sliced, hulled strawberries

¼ cup plus 3 tablespoons sugar

2 cups flour

½ teaspoon salt

1 tablespoon baking powder

½ cup butter

1 egg, beaten

⅔ cup milk

Whipped Cream Filling (recipe follows)

Place the strawberries in a bowl and sprinkle with ¼ cup sugar; set aside. Mix the dry ingredients in a large bowl with a whisk. Add the butter and cut it in with a pastry cutter until crumbly. In a small bowl, mix the egg and the milk together. Pour over the crumbled mixture and stir just enough to moisten.

Spread this into a greased 8-inch cake pan, and bake at 450°F for 15 minutes, or until done. Allow the cake to cool in the pan for 10 minutes, then remove it. When cool enough to handle, cut the cake in half horizontally. Spread a layer of the whipped cream filling on the cake, then a layer of the strawberries. Put the top on the cake and frost with the remaining whipped cream filling and strawberries.

Recipe adapted from the *California Recipe Book*, 1872

WHIPPED CREAM FILLING

MAKES 2 CUPS

2 cups whipping cream

⅓ cup sugar

Beat the whipping cream in a large bowl with an electric mixer at high speed.

Add the sugar and beat until soft peaks form.

A large procession of children and adults walk down the center of the street in Boise, Idaho, carrying American flags and placards. Crowds of spectators line the downtown streets (ca. 1900s). COURTESY OF THE LIBRARY OF CONGRESS

Recipe adapted from the *Fredericksburg* (Texas) *Home Kitchen Cook Book*, 1916

GOOSEBERRY PIE

MAKES 1 PIE

4 cups fresh gooseberries

⅔ cup sugar

¼ cup flour

⅛ teaspoon salt

1 tablespoon cold butter, cut into pieces

1 recipe for Piecrust (recipe follows), unbaked

Snip the ends off the gooseberries. In a large bowl, combine the berries, sugar, flour, and salt. Mix well.

Line a 9-inch pie pan with 1 crust and fill with the berry mixture. Dot the top with the butter and cover with second piecrust; seal. Make four or five slits in the top crust to allow the steam to escape. Bake at 375°F for 45 minutes. If the crust starts to brown, cover it with aluminum foil. Cool completely before cutting.

Note: Blueberries can be substituted.

Recipe adapted from the *Fredericksburg* (Texas) *Home Kitchen Cook Book*, 1916

PIECRUST

MAKES 2 CRUSTS

4 cups flour

½ teaspoon salt

1 tablespoon baking powder

1 cup butter or lard

¾ cup water, plus more as needed

Combine the flour, salt, and baking powder in a large bowl. Cut in the butter with a pastry cutter or two knives until the butter is pebble size. Add the water and mix until blended. Add more water a few drops at a time, if needed.

Mix just enough to form a ball. Wrap in plastic wrap and chill for about an hour, if possible. Roll crust out on a floured surface, turning it often so the pastry doesn't stick.

Recipe adapted from the *Fredericksburg* (Texas) *Home Kitchen Cook Book*, 1916

CHAPTER FIVE

THANKSGIVING

"THIS IS THANKSGIVING, WHICH IS CELEBRATED BY US BY PARTAK-ing of a dinner of wild ducks roasted, stewed quails, mince pie and a very fine watermelon just picked from the vines, all of which we heartily enjoyed." It's odd to see watermelon mentioned with Thanksgiving, but that's what California gold rush–country merchant Stephen Chapin David recalled having in 1853.

What pioneers ate really depended upon where they lived. There were traditional items, but regional items were often featured on frontier tables. Thanksgiving was celebrated all over the frontier, with many traditional eighteenth-century New

A JOYOUS THANKSGIVING DAY

Thankful for every blessing. Your heart brimful of cheer

Turkeys have been long associated with Thanksgiving. Like today, they also appeared on postcards and greeting cards (ca. 1900s). SHERRY MONAHAN

England items appearing on restaurant and home tables alike. They had turkey, goose, cranberry sauce, pumpkins, pies, and all the trimmings similar to today's. Thanksgiving was a time for families to get together for a few days of eating, games, and fun. It was a holiday where thanks were given to God for the fall harvest and other blessings.

Thanksgiving has changed over the decades, but people have been giving thanks for bountiful harvests since the Pilgrims did in 1621. In 1631 the Massachusetts Bay colony had a Thanksgiving in February to express their delight in provisions they desperately needed. In 1704 the English governor of the Massachusetts colony proclaimed, "Order and appoint Thursday the twenty-third of this present November a day of general THANKSGIVING throughout this Province, inhibiting all Sarville Labour thereupon; and exhorting both Ministers and people in their respective congregations, to celebrate the praises of GOD, for all HIS benefits and Blessings, and to devote themselves a Thank-Offering to Him in a right ordered conversation."

While Thanksgiving proclamations were issued by presidents going back to George Washington, there was no national celebration. Western pioneers began making this a big festivity shortly after Lincoln declared Thanksgiving an official holiday in 1863. On October 3, 1863, he wrote, "The year that is drawing towards its close, has been filled with the blessings of fruitful fields and healthful skies. To these bounties, which are so constantly enjoyed that we are prone to forget the source from which they come, others have been added, which are of so extraordinary a nature, that they cannot fail to penetrate and soften even the heart which is habitually insensible to the ever-watchful providence of Almighty God."

Even before President Lincoln made that proclamation, American Elizabeth LeBreton Gunn celebrated Thanksgiving while she was living in Sonora, Mexico, from 1851 to 1861. Despite not having a complete traditional meal, she and her family celebrated Thanksgiving. She penned a letter to family back home about it: "Now I must tell you about Thanksgiving. I baked six pumpkin and two cranberry pies on Wednesday. The berries came from Oregon and were good, but small. They are two dollars a gallon [about thirty-nine dollars in today's money]. I put currants in the pumpkin pies and they were very nice, but not like yours, because I cannot afford the milk and eggs and our hens do not lay now. I also made a boiled bread pudding with raisins in it. On Thanksgiving Day, I baked a 'rooster pie,' and Lewis and the children said it was delightful." She and her husband Lewis were both longtime abolitionists, ran the *Sonora Herald*, and owned a drugstore. Lewis was also involved in keeping California a free state.

Another pioneer penned a letter home about her Thanksgiving in Lawrence, Kansas. In 1856, pioneers Edward and Sara Fitch wrote to their parents, who were living back in Massachusetts:

> We had a very good time Thanksgiving. Do you remember that once a number of years ago you had a turkey at Thanksgiving? The only turkey that I ever knew you to have and do you remember that we did not like it and voted that turkey was not half as good as chicken? Well I have had a prejudice against turkey ever since and thot I should not like it but this year I conquered my prejudice and bought a turkey for dinner. We had it baked and it was first rate. Our family of that day consisted of Father W. Brother

George, and a young friend he brot with him from Topeka, Mr & Mrs Hanscom (It was the first Thanksgiving dinner she ever ate, she being a New Yorker and always having kept Christmas), Sarah, our three children and last but not least a young man whom you may have known at some former period of life—named Edward Payson. We did up the dinner after the most approved style, said dinner consisting of turkey with stuffing, sweet and Irish potatoes, onions, & cranberry sauce, mince, grape, squash, & Whortleberry pies of Sarah's best make. You can imagine they were good when I tell you that the day before Thanksgiving she had 35 pies and Sunday after there were but 4 left—so we think she is a pretty good cook. [The writing changes here to Sarah's.] You may accept that as one of Edward's stories—in the first place I only baked 25 and instead of 4 left there were 10 & 5 of those that disappeared were taken away whole— so you see we were not such enormous eaters as one might infer from E's statements. Mine you may depend upon as fact. I wish you had all been here to enjoy our dinner with us—we would have all been willing to sit close—and keep our elbows down—to make room for four more plates—poor little Georgie—I said four more plates—Georgie should had an extra one in the very first place with an extra share of plums in his pudding. [Writing is again Edward's.] Sarah has been trying to make out that I have been telling a yarn but when I tell you that George and his friend stayed till Sat. noon and that George is as great a hand for pie as I am (you used to know something about that when you always had to hide the pies away from me) and when I tell you that every time we were in the house we were eating pie you will take her statement with some grains of allowance or at least think she may have made a mistake when she tried to write the number of pies we had, for the other is what she told me or I understood. In the evening we had a social time singing and playing chess & chequers, eating cream & jelly cakes, apples & nuts (that were not eat) and drinking wine, real good grape wine, of our own make and I think about equal to that currant wine that you bragged so much on when we were East. And if we had only had two or three bottles of your cider we would have discussed the question whether (John A. Fitch) (Ethan Griffons) cider was *not fully equal to wine, which question might have been decided the way the liquor was strongest. But as we were all able to walk straight after a night's sleep I think the wine was pretty good. So much for what we eat on Thanksgiving and as eating seems to be the great thing on that day we must have had a good Thanksgiving.*

While some pioneers enjoyed a quiet meal with friends and families, others enjoyed dining out and attending parties and balls. Thanksgiving balls were pleasant affairs, with dancing, laughter, and dining. One such event took place in Vermillion, South Dakota. The *Dakota Republican* reported, "Never did we attend a more happy occasion than the Ball of Thursday evening last. The company composed as it was of all the grace, beauty, and loveliness of which this city boasts, was the most pleasant, neatly attired, yes, richly dressed party that has ever graced the halls of St. Nicholas." The Masonic Hall in Port Townsend, Washington, also had an elegant Thanksgiving ball, and resident Barney O'Ragan was so elated with it, he wrote to the local paper:

An it was a grand affair, entirely. . . . At the ball I saw wonders there. Every man's wife in this town was there but mine, and the reason why she did not attend was, because I couldn't find her; knowingly speaking, I never saw her myself. The ladies looked gay and the men bully. All went in for diversion, and they had lots of it. Out-side the night was stormy, but inside it's little we cared for the national debt. We had good music, which was furnished by Mr. Edward L. Jones and his string band. The dancing was kept up until early next morning. The ladies in attendance were elegantly dressed, and displayed more real taste than you will generally find in small towns on this coast. Sociability and geniality were the order of the night, and everyone seemed to feel happy—no doubt because I did. The subject of women suffrage was never mentioned, nor did I see a man with a black eye in the hall.* . . . But this seems to be stringing out, and unless I stop, where will I end, not, I fear, until the next ball; so the managers of this, *the finest* ball ever given in Port Townsend, I wish every success in the future.*

The editor of the *Weekly Argus* did not share his sentiments, and he placed this note at the bottom of Mr. O'Ragan's letter:

*Mr. O'Ragan's ideas of a pleasant Thanksgiving reunion seem to be confused. The gentleman congratulates the managers of the nonappearance of a "black eye!" Barney, in the hight of this inspiration, remembered the "Tim Finnigan" wakes of his native "isle of the sea," and missed the distinctive badge here. You'll like the change, Barney—when you are accustomed to it.—Editor.

San Quentin isn't exactly the place where people attended balls, but in 1877 the prison took on a ball-like setting with flags, flowers, and evergreen decorations for a Thanksgiving-eve ball. The prisoners provided the entertainment as they played violins, guitars, accordions, and banjos. Since the crowd was male only, four of the prisoners dressed in borrowed female attire for the dances. Many attended Thanksgiving services at the prison chapel, and later they enjoyed a performance from the prison choir and listened to the usual speeches. Thanksgiving dinner consisted of roasted mutton, roasted pork, apples, peas, pies, and cakes.

Green Corn Ceremony

Centuries before the Anglos landed in America, the Cherokee Indians celebrated their version of Thanksgiving with their "green corn ceremony." Green corn, or any type of green produce, was a way to differentiate between fresh and dried. According to the Cherokee Nation Cultural Resource Center,

> *The Cherokees were raising corn as early as 1,000 BC. Before European contact the Cherokees were already participating in a thanksgiving ceremony; the most important ceremony of the year, called the "Green Corn Ceremony." This traditional dance and festival was a very important event for the Cherokees. It was the beginning of the New Year; a time when our ancestors gave thanks for the corn crop that they saw as a continued life for them. It was a time for forgiveness and for grudges to be left behind—a time to begin anew. A part of their celebration was fasting, then gathering at the ceremonial grounds to play stickball, dance and have a big feast.*

Football

It's true that pie and turkey are synonymous with Thanksgiving, but so is football. Yes, even back in the nineteenth century, pioneers played football on Thanksgiving. In 1885 Kansas City, Missouri, residents, some three hundred of them, enjoyed a Thanksgiving Day football game. Early American football was a cross between rugby and today's American football, but no one officiated the game. Each team consisted of eleven players, including a quarterback, rushers, half backs, and full backs. The *Kansas City Times* reported,

> *About 300 half-frozen spectators assembled at the baseball grounds to witness the match game of football between Monges and Gruber elevens. As an exhibition of skill,*

the game was not a brilliant one, but as a mirth-producing spectacle it was a howling success. It would be difficult to state by just what rules the match was governed, but as near as could be determined they were a combination of Marquis of Queensbury, go as you please and catch as can catch. . . . The Monges team were arrayed in the gorgeous crimson knees breeches of the Kansas City ball club, while the Grubers were resplendent in black jersey caps and blue flannel shirts. The trifling formality of an umpire being dispensed with.

After nearly two hours they called it a draw at six each because both teams were too beat up or too tired to continue.

Playing football on Thanksgiving is a long tradition (1902). COURTESY OF THE LIBRARY OF CONGRESS

Osage Indian School football team in Oklahoma, 1909. COURTESY OF THE LIBRARY OF CONGRESS

By 1889 football had become more like the traditional game that is played today. However, it was clear that most players and spectators didn't know what to expect, and in Omaha, Nebraska, on November 26, 1889, the *World Herald* wrote about the game played on Thanksgiving Day: "Football is only beginning to make its way west, but it is a game par excellence for the fall of the year. It is quick and exciting, full of surprises and comical mishaps. Every person who witnesses the game will be delighted with it."

Restaurant Fare

Football wasn't the only big hit in Kansas City, Missouri, because the hotel chefs there outdid themselves. Items on the local hotel menus included bluepoint oysters, littleneck clams, pâté de foie gras, red snapper, black bass, salmon, capon, turkey, duck, ribs of beef, veal quail stuffed with truffles, elk, squirrel, opossum, shrimp, pompano, asparagus, artichokes, puddings, pies, ice cream, macaroons, and Roquefort and Edam cheeses.

Kansas City wasn't the only Missouri town to offer delicious Thanksgiving viands. St. Louis's Lindell Hotel, the largest in the city at the time, offered an extensive menu. It included bluepoint oysters on the half shell and green turtle, Victoria consommé, and chicken bouillon soups. Other pre-main courses included croquettes of oysters, Russian caviar, salted almonds, radishes, and branch celery. The main course selections were extensive:

Baked red snapper à la matelote normande with potatoes hollandaise and claret wine

Boiled leg of mutton with caper sauce

Philadelphia capon with pork and celery sauce

Baron of beef au jus with mashed potatoes

Young turkey with oyster dressing and roasted sweet potatoes

Mongol goose with applesauce and cauliflower

Filet de beouf, à la Trianon with string beans

Pattie of sweet breads, à la Toulouse with petit pois and queen fritters with vanilla sauce

Roast red head duck with currant jelly

Salads included chicken, lettuce, watercress, and lobster.

The desserts offered were English plum pudding with hard and cognac sauce, mince pie, chocolate cream caramels, pumpkin pie, gâteau assortis, vanilla meringue tarts, charlotte russe, and Nesselrode ice cream.

The Sherman House in Aberdeen, South Dakota, offered patrons and residents bluepoint oysters with sliced lemon, gumbo à la Creole, consommé royale, queen olives from Spain, and celery to start. Main dishes included the following:

Baked salmon stuffed with oysters and potato pancakes

Boiled chicken and salt pork

Salmi of blue teal duck

Stuffed rabbit with brown gravy

Scalloped oysters with cream puffs and red wine sauce

Roast spring turkey stuffed with chestnuts and cranberry sauce

Roast prime sirloin of beef with mushrooms

Roast haunch of venison with raspberry jelly

Saddle of Kentucky lamb à la barbecue

Other dishes included boned turkey, homemade headcheese, prairie chicken salad, cream salad, mashed potatoes, sweet potatoes, Hubbard squash, French peas, and sugar corn. For dessert patrons chose from English plum pudding with brandy sauce, mince pie, pumpkin pie, whipped cream, strawberry pie, port wine or brandy jelly, Neapolitan ice cream, fruit, hickory nuts, cream, and chocolate cakes. Also available were apples, bananas, oranges, and mixed nuts. Beverages included iced tea, tea, coffee, chocolate, and milk.

Offering fish, seafood, and other delicacies in locations that don't have an ocean was easy because most of it came from a can, as long as you had regular supply shipments. Many mercantile stores, like Falk-Bloch in Idaho, were offering bluepoint and Wagner's oysters, mackerel, salmon, herring, sardines, shrimp, Russian caviar, clams, and codfish for its residents and hotels in 1892. Portland, Oregon, took advantage of its local bounty and offered Columbia River salmon in addition to all the traditional dished served on Thanksgiving.

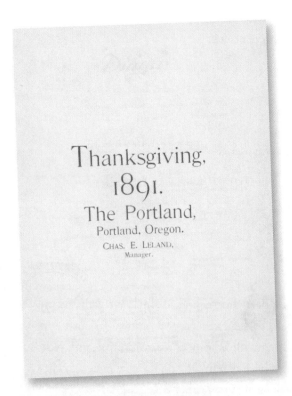

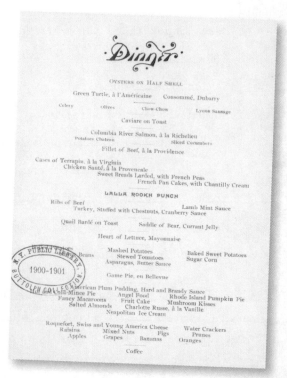

The Hotel Portland offered a grand Thanksgiving meal in 1891. The menu included local and traditional dishes including salmon, turkey, quail, mashed potatoes, sweet potatoes, corn, and pumpkin and mince pies. COURTESY OF THE NEW YORK PUBLIC LIBRARY

Community Events

Hotels and restaurants offered Thanksgiving meals, but so did civic and charitable organizations. San Francisco, California's Salvation Army offered a turkey banquet and parade on Thanksgiving Day. The soldiers' reunion took place at Barracks No. 2 at the corner of Sacramento and Kearny Streets. Major and Mrs. Keppel, the couple in charge, offered an informal and cordial welcome to all at 10:30 a.m. The *San Francisco Chronicle* wrote of Major Keppel, "After thanking the several hundred men by whom he was received he concluded a brief address by advising them to be obedient, willing, loyal and active soldiers in the service of the Lord."

From 12:30 to 2:30 p.m., a banquet was held at Congress Hall on Market Street. Over five hundred "poor but respectable appearing" men, women, and children enjoyed roast turkey, cranberry sauce, mince pie, fruit, cake, and more. They served fifty turkeys that weighed between seven and nineteen pounds each. At 4:00 p.m., a turkey parade was organized, and various bands, a giant "turkey," costumed waiters, and a man carrying a carving knife marched down the main street to everyone's delight.

The Ladies Art League in Newton, Kansas, gave an annual Tissue Paper Ball on Thanksgiving, as they had for some years. At 9:00 p.m. on Thanksgiving evening in 1893, the ball was opened when the

THE SALVATION ARMY'S TURKEY PARADE.

This Salvation Army Thanksgiving turkey ad appeared in the San Francisco Chronicle *on November 25, 1892. SAN FRANCISCO CHRONICLE, NOVEMBER 25, 1892*

local orchestra played the first march. A total of twenty-four marches were played and the dancers took their places and twirled to them all. Tissue-paper costumes included a variety of items like butterflies, clover leaves, lilies, tulips, mums, and the American flag. Prizes were awarded in both a lady's and gentlemen's category for the most artistic costume. After the dancing was complete, the ladies of the Catholic church served a traditional supper to the hungry participants.

Fraternal organizations, churches, fire and police departments, unions, companies, and charities all hosted balls, usually costumed, on Thanksgiving evening. Like most balls of the time, they offered music for dancing, prizes for the best or most unique costumes, and provided supper. Towns in South Dakota, Idaho, Washington, Montana, Colorado, and Iowa held balls like these. While these events were popular during the nineteenth century, Thanksgiving became less about being thankful to God for the harvest and more about ways to celebrate the harvest as the turn of the century neared. The costume parties and balls lasted for a while, but eventually they faded away when other forms of entertainment, like movies, replaced them.

Christmas Shopping

Believe it or not, shopping's association with Thanksgiving is not a new thing. Even though merchants advertised Thanksgiving-related items stores and merchants took the opportunity to offer a variety of merchandise for sale. Newspapers across the West contained Christmas advertisements. The *Daily Nebraska Press* ran this ad in the late 1800s: "The Governor's Thanksgiving Proclamation reminds us that turkeys are a good thing to have—so are pictures from Howard's." In addition to Howard's, stores across the West promoted everything from clothing to household wares. Clarksville, Texas's *Standard* advertised, "Don't forget Thompson's patent flour for your Christmas cakes" and "Come where my love has dreaming, and let's go 'round to Thompson's and get our Christmas

Whisky." Ads for Christmas cards, fine china, cut glass, stationery, jewelry, dolls, toys, books, pictures, and more appeared.

On November 25, 1892, Marston's in San Diego advertised,

> *Between Thanksgiving and Christmas come the busy days. Then is the time when the well-equipped store is appreciated by busy men and women. "Things" are wanted, a thousand and one things. His store that has them has the business. It seems to be the settled fact that Marston's is that store in San Diego. There complete and full-furnished stocks—Dry Goods, Carpets and Men's Furnishings—each one the largest of its class in the city. . . . We call special attention to the varied assortment of articles in our Men's Department that are holiday gifts. The success of our holiday sales last year in this department has led us to make better preparations this season. Take a look early before the freshest and best are culled out.*

Sales promotions also took the form of parades in some frontier towns, and in 1909 the *Independence* (Kansas) *Daily Star* announced, "The parade for the big Sales Day will be formed at 10:30 sharp. . . . All parties who are going to take part in the parade are requested to be present and not to delay the forming of the line. McCray's band, the best in the state will lead the parade." The next day the same paper ran this: "Special Thanksgiving Offering. Thanksgiving is now at hand—the day when a man takes pride in his dress. There will be Church Services, the Foot Ball Game, Feasting, Family Reunions and a general good time. Possibly your wardrobe is not as complete as you would like to have it. If so, we have prepared for the event, specially, by offering you any of our $25.00 suits or overcoats at this week's special $20.00"

On November 23, 1910, the *Oregonian* in Portland placed many ads in anticipation of the Christmas holiday. The real estate firm of Messrs. Mead and Murray advertised, "Your wife's Christmas Gift—It's not too soon to be thinking about it. Let it be a good gift this

San Francisco children were already anticipating Christmas in early November when this ad appeared in the paper on November 12, 1905. SAN FRANCISCO CHRONICLE, NOVEMBER 12, 1905

year—a deed of one of those ideal home sites in Laurelhurst! Take your wife to see Laurelhurst now; it will be a revelation to you both. Then on Christmas surprise her with a deed to the lot she liked best. Will it make her happy? You know it!" Next to their ad appeared one for the J. K. Gill Company that promoted their sectional bookcases as the perfect gift for wives, husbands, children, relatives, and friends.

Aberdeen, South Dakota's *Daily News* had ads for shopping and for dining in 1894. The town took advantage of its bountiful shipments that had been received in time for Thanksgiving.

As the turn of the century neared, merchant associations all over the West encouraged local businessmen to push the Christmas season sales the day after Thanksgiving. While some of this started in the latter 1800s, newspaper ads became more frequent. Some merchants even placed half- and full-page ads. In 1896 the *Kansas City Star* advertised, "The Beautiful Christmas Number of St. Nicholas is now ready. 'A Christmas in Bethlehem,' richly illustrated. A poem by Mary Mapes Dodge. 'A Boy I Knew,' by Laurence Hamilton, 'The Voyage of the Northern Light,' by J. T. Trowbridge, A St. Nicholas Christmas Card. A Snowbound Christmas, etc. etc. Do not fail to buy this number on a newsstand (25 cents)." An ad for the December edition of *Harper's* magazine appeared right next to this one, and it was outlined in holly leaves instead of the typical straight lines. On November 22, 1897, the *Oregonian* in Portland ran this ad for merchants Olds & King: "Start the Christmas Trading Now.

Will help both you and us—you by giving us ample time for selecting; Us by giving us the opportunity to serve you carefully. The hurrying, pushing crowds of a few weeks later will make satisfactory trading harder for both of us. Special inducements to holiday buying this week."

While merchants didn't regularly push the Christmas shopping season until after Thanksgiving, there were some who did it in the middle to late 1800s. Hale Brothers department store in San Francisco boldly placed a Christmas ad in the *Chronicle* on November 12, 1905, and included Santa Claus. This was the third year in a row they held their Santa Claus content. They also took the opportunity to tease and tempt the children with a grand toy ad.

In addition to the local restaurants placing notices in the paper to tantalize the palates of its readers, society pages reported private events—birthday parties, reunions, anniversaries, and holiday parties—in detail. The Journal in Sioux City, Iowa, dedicated page ten of its 1897 paper to nothing but parties. The headline simply read "Society." The notices for Thanksgiving parties included the names of the host, guests, and what time dinner was served. Other notices announced who left town and where they went for the holiday.

Songs and poems aren't typically associated with Thanksgiving in the twenty-first century, but they were popular in the nineteenth century.

 "A Thanksgiving Song"

Thanksgiving, for you, dear! A sweet thanksgiving

For what you were in all the past to me;

For what you are—a joy that sweetens living.

For that you are to be!

Thanksgiving for those eyes—the kind, the splendid!

Dear eyes, whose light the whole wide world would miss;

Your voice, in which all melodies are blended—

Thanksgiving for your kiss!

Thanksgiving for your smile, like sunlight streaming

Over the heart which still for you must beat;

Dear, if to love you but be idle dreaming.

Never was dream so sweet!

Thanksgiving for you, dear—the sweetly human;

Gentle, but brave, with kindliest deeds and words;

How the world blossoms for a little woman—

How smile the meadows and how sing the birds!

Thanksgiving is the sweetest song and story

For love that lives when life in darkness dies;

For love that crowns life—death—with endless glory

And lights the golden pathway to the skies!

Denver Post, November 28, 1895

"The Happy Gleaners," a Thanksgiving song, appeared in several western papers in the 1890s. WEEKLY CAPITAL, TOPEKA, KANSAS, NOVEMBER 27, 1890

Theodore Roosevelt, who spent a great deal of time in the West, felt Thanksgiving should not be influenced by current trends (which included football decor), either in the food eaten or the way a home was decorated. He believed the trendy French food popular at the time was a deplorable way to celebrate an American holiday. He decorated the White House with cornstalks, fruit leaves, dried grasses, and flowers that were "used at the early Thanksgiving celebrations." They also used old Indian relics and anything suggestive of colonial times and pictures depicting colonial scenes.

Holiday Decor

The *Salt Lake Herald* and the *Dallas Morning News* ran ads for linens and furniture to improve your Thanksgiving holiday in Thanksgiving papers in 1905. The *Star Telegram* in Dallas's neighbor Fort Worth offered suggestions on how to decorate for the family-oriented holiday. Correspondent Edith Brown began,

> *The very close of the month of November brings Thanksgiving and the well-stored grain houses and general prosperity of the nation attest its right and duly give thanks. . . . On these days, too, the annual football games at colleges marking the close of the football season attract the young and old college folks and Thanksgiving is a busy day. Whether the family only are the guests at the dinner table or there are friends to join the family circle, the day should receive its homage—not only in the serving of the turkey but in*

the decoration of the table. . . . For decorations for Thanksgiving are always the turkeys, the chrysanthemums and the footballs, but for the hostess who desires an idea a bit more elaborate than any of these there are the ancient goddesses of myths to draw upon. For the centerpieces have a great mound of purple grapes and wheat. The sheaves of wheat in the natural state may be somewhat difficult to secure at this time of year, but if so the artificial sheaves with which hats are trimmed will serve the purpose quite as well. The beauty of this decoration need not be dwelt upon, for a little imagination will picture it. The wild grape vine or bunches of artificial grapes trimmed with dark blue ribbon may be caught to the chandelier and draped at two corners of the table; wheat, caught together like a vine, falling from the chandelier to the other two corners. At the four corners the vines twine, slightly, about small statuettes of Ceres, the goddess of agriculture and civilization, Prosperina, the goddess of vegetation; Diana, the goddess of chase, and Fortuna, the goddess of plenty. The four goddesses may bear the four candles, shaded with purple and yellow shades—two in each color. The place cards may be small contributions like those laid at the feet of the four goddesses—a candy deer, to represent Diana; a sheaf of wheat for Ceres; fruits or vegetables for Prosperina, and horns of plenty for Fortuna. . . .

. . . Another and more American-like decoration may be found in the use of candy box turkeys which strut about the confectioners' windows these days. An immense turkey for the center may hold in her beak long strands of narrow red, white, and blue ribbon. At the end of each strand have a small turkey bearing the place card in its beak. For another turkey decoration, the strands may come from beneath the turkey at the neck. A small American flag will serve as the place card. At the close of the meal each diner will be requested to draw a strand of the ribbon from the turkey. At the end of the ribbon he will find a blank sheet of paper and a small pencil. At the top of the paper will be found written a quotation descriptive of the guest for him it is intended, and beneath will be written, "Count your many blessing, Name them one by one." Thereupon every member

of the party must set about putting down on the paper the things for which he is thank-ful. At the close of the time allotted to the contest the hostess passes a great cup bearing the inscription, "My cup overflows." The slips of papers are put in this and the one who has found the greatest number of blessings for which thanks are returned is given a prize—the turkey is served as the center piece, filled with candy, for instance. For the

Even in the nineteenth century, stores advertised holiday items at Thanksgiving. This one appeared in the Dallas Morning News *in 1905.* DALLAS MORNING NEWS, NOVEMBER 2, 1905

Salt Lake City residents were encouraged to shop for linens and other items as they prepared for their Thanksgiving celebrations. This ad appeared in the Salt Lake Herald *on November 19, 1905.* SALT LAKE HERALD, NOVEMBER 19, 1905

young folk, a decoration of footballs is good. The center may be a large ball carried by Minerva, symbolizing victory, or the football may surmount a mound of flowers in the colors of the winning team for whom the luncheon is given or the one with which the young people are allied. The place cards should be small footballs tied with the ribbons of the team represented.

Wichita, Kansas's *Searchlight* also provided readers with some ideas for decorations and favors in 1905. They began, "Observance of national holidays is not considered complete in these days of inventiveness without the introduction of decorations or favors particularly agreeable to the occasion. Thanksgiving being a festival time, offers a special opportunity for the favor designs. And the shops teem with novelties suggestive of the day and its time-honored manner of observance. This being football season the hero of the gridiron and his famous leather sphere serve also as models for favors and decorative adjuncts and these mementos are found side by side with the distinctively Thanksgiving souvenirs and share popularity with the latter." They reported that while most souvenirs were inexpensive, hostesses felt the need to spend a great deal of money on centerpiece or party favors. They blamed the excess expense on the many choices she had.

An elegant greeting for the holiday (ca. 1900s)
SHERRY MONAHAN

Entertaining Guests

There were many ways to entertain guests after the grand feast, and they included cards, dancing, music, and games. The *Idaho Statesman* suggested some games a host could offer her guests in 1905. They reported, "The Thanksgiving dinner with its time-honored menu

Thanksgiving Centerpieces

Wichita, Kansas's *Searchlight* offered these designs for a centerpiece in 1905: "For instance, she [hostess] might select the football centerpiece pictured above with a mass of chrysanthemums rising from the center. The flowers are realistically fashioned from crepe paper and all the hues of the natural blossom are produced. Then there is the candy box, with its top of chrysanthemum petals, colored in the various college tints and appropriately letter or the football in leather hue, and the box on which [it] is mounted a papier mache collegian, togged in full regalia and grasping a football."

They also suggested a basket that is woven from wheat stalks and filled with red and yellow colored fruit. Matching chrysanthemums and candles, along with a big yellow chiffon ribbon entwined with smilax, would complete the table.

which time out of mind has included the national bird, pumpkin pie and the rest of the good things that we know by heart is easily provided by the good housewife. As for the bad one on this day of rejoicing it would be hard indeed were she to experiment on her family and guests. But the question of how to amuse her guests, who are apt to be of varying ages, confronts even the experienced hostess."

Papers all over the West continued to fill their pages with suggestions on games, decor, and what to eat. North Dakota's *Grand Forks Herald* suggested a menu for the hostess

Drawing Turkeys: Each player is given a blank sheet of paper and a pencil. They are then blindfolded and required to draw a turkey. When the designated time is up, they are to remove their blindfolds, write their names of the back of the paper and place them in a basket. Three judges who did not play are charged with choosing a winner.

who not only served dinner at her house but also who had guests staying for a few days. The article began "The great festival of this month in America is Thanksgiving Day. It is handed down from colonial times, originated in New England and was first observed there, but now in almost every state in the republic. November, stormy and dismal is its weather, shines forth as a jewel among the months from this great festival of gratitude to God and love and reunion in hearts and homes. Thanksgiving is wholly American in origin, and with what thoughts shall American women concentrate to the elevation and betterment of their lives."

The article suggested menus for all three meals: "Dinner is the most formal of our three meals, and a dinner for

An elegant greeting for the holiday (ca. 1900s). SHERRY MONAHAN

Turk-he Game: Make a huge turban of newspaper and draw names to see who will wear it first. The first person to wear the turban is called "His Sublime Highness the Great Turk he." The Turk he marshals all the players into a half circle before him. He begins to ask questions of his "subjects" using certain key words or omitting them. If the Turk he uses the words *and, if, why, will,* or *don't* in his or her question, then the subject being asked should remain silent. If the Turk he's question contains none of those words, then the subject must answer the question. The pace of the game is fast, and the first person to answer at the wrong time is instructed to perform a ridiculous act as ordered by His Sublime Highness.

a large company is quite an undertaking, especially where the home family is small and the meal must be prepared by one pair of hands. To all such I would advise, limit your ambition, or get someone to help you through the undertaking—perhaps the wisest policy would be to do both. Anyway, don't treat your guests to 'stewed hostess' or one so wearied by preparation and much serving as to make them feel guilty of having been the innocent means of her undue exertions."

For breakfast, they suggested fruit, oatmeal, hamburg steak with Delmonico potatoes, drop biscuits, and coffee. For the main dinner meal, which was served around noon, they offered a choice of two menus. The first one included raw oyster consommé, roast turkey with giblet gravy, baked sweet potatoes, creamed onions, cranberry sauce, stewed corn, celery salad, cheese fingers, pumpkin and mince pies. The second suggestion included oysters on the half shell, salted pecans, clear soup with quenelles, roast turkey with celery and

When family and friends couldn't be together on the frontier, they shared postcards like this one (ca. 1900s). SHERRY MONAHAN

nut stuffing, cranberry sauce, corn, sweet potato croquettes, baked ham, spinach, dressed lettuce, cheese straws, pumpkin pie, and baked Indian corn pudding. After having such a huge meal at lunchtime, they offered a light menu for supper, which was the traditional term for meals served in the evening. They suggested celery salad in a jelly border served with biscuits, preserves, cake, and coffee.

Perfume Game: In 1905, the *Idaho Statesman* offered this game for hostesses expecting Thanksgiving guests:

> A perfume game is one of the latest forms of entertainment. After the guests have arrived the lights are turned out and the guests are seating in a circle around the room, or better still, close together around a big table. Perfect silence is observed and at first there is a feeling of "spookiness" which suggests all sorts of weird performances. Then the hostess, who sits at one end of the table, hands a bottle to her neighbor with whispered instructions to take a whiff of the contents and pass it along. The bottles are passed in rapid succession one after another, each one containing something like cologne, different essences, toilet vinegars, or any other liquid that is not to disagreeable. When about fifteen bottles have been passed the lights are turned up and the guests are required to write down the names of as many odors as they can remember. Of course they are not told how many bottles have been passed. A prize is offered for the best list. This might take the form of an old fashioned bouquet.

A Forgotten Tradition

An odd and now-forgotten Thanksgiving tradition was celebrated all over the country in the late nineteenth and early twentieth centuries: masquerade balls and parades. It was common for children and adults to wear masks, as is done on Halloween today. In 1902 the *Greene Recorder* in Iowa ran a story called "False Faces." It began,

Thanksgiving time is the busiest season for the manufacturers of and dealers in masks and false faces. The fantastical costume parades and the old custom of masking and dressing for amusement on Thanksgiving Day keep up from year to year in many parts of the country, so that the quantity of false faces sold at this season is enormous. The manufacturers make it a point to get up new styles, and this year brownies, "yaller kids," parrot visages and many other novelties will be on sale. Masks of prominent men and the foremost political leaders are made by some manufacturers, and large sized false hands, noses, ear, etc. are also new and amusing.

Thanksgiving Recipes from the Old West

These recipes and food are suggested by the Victorian pioneers themselves. They include foods that are traditional Thanksgiving dishes still today and a few that aren't. Both fish and turkey were popular meals on the frontier.

BRAISED RED SNAPPER

SERVES 2–4

¼ cup flour

Salt and pepper to taste

1 pound red snapper fillets

Pinch of thyme

Pinch of summer savory

1 bay leaf

1 (8-ounce) can tomatoes or 1 cup fresh tomatoes, chopped

1 lemon, sliced

2 tablespoons butter

Sprinkle an ovenproof pan with flour, salt, and pepper. Arrange the fish on this. Sprinkle the fish with salt, pepper, thyme, and summer savory. Add the bay leaf to one of the fillets.

Pour the tomatoes evenly over the fish and add a lemon slice and a dot of butter. Bake at 350°F for 20 minutes, or until the fish flakes.

Recipe adapted from Denver's *Daily News*, March 13, 1908

SALMON À LA CREOLE

SERVES 2-4

2 pounds salmon, cut into serving pieces

Salt and freshly ground pepper

4 tablespoons butter

1 tablespoon oil

2 slices bacon, chopped

2 cups chopped tomatoes or 3 large tomatoes, chopped

1 bell pepper, chopped

1 small onion, chopped

Season the salmon with ½ teaspoon salt and a ¼ teaspoon pepper. Melt the butter and oil in an ovenproof skillet (cast iron works great) over high heat. When the butter bubbles, add the salmon and brown quickly on both sides. Place the skillet in a 450°F oven and bake for 5 to 8 minutes, depending on the thickness of the salmon. When done, a fork should pierce the center of the salmon easily.

While the salmon is cooking, sauté the bacon in a frying pan for about 5 minutes. Add the tomatoes, peppers, onion, and salt and pepper to taste. Cook over medium heat for about 5 minutes and then reduce the heat to simmer. Cover and cook until sauce-like, about 20 minutes.

Place the salmon on a platter or individual plates and pour some of the sauce over the salmon.

Recipe adapted from Jonesboro, Arkansas's *Daily Times-Enterprise*, September 15, 1904

YOUNG TURKEY WITH OYSTER DRESSING

SERVES 8–10

One 12–15 pound turkey

Oyster Dressing (recipe follows)

2 tablespoons butter, softened

Preheat the oven to 350°F. Remove any excess fat from the cavity of the bird and discard. Set the giblets, neck, heart, and liver aside. Rinse and dry the turkey inside and out. Stuff the cavity and the neck area with the oyster dressing. Once stuffed, truss the neck area, then the cavity. Before cutting your string, be sure to wrap the legs as well.

Rub the butter all over the bird. Place the turkey in a large covered roasting pan. Be sure to baste the bird every 30 to 40 minutes, until done. To obtain a golden color, remove the lid 30 minutes before cooking time is up. A bird this size should take approximately 3¾ to 4½ hours to cook. Your turkey is done when the temperature with a meat thermometer is 180°F in thigh and 165°F in breast or stuffing.

OYSTER DRESSING

MAKES ENOUGH FOR A 12–15 POUND TURKEY

4 cups homemade croutons

8 tablespoons butter

1 cup onion, minced

¼ cup celery, minced

Turkey liver, minced (optional)

1 teaspoon fresh parsley, chopped

1 teaspoon salt

Freshly ground pepper to taste

1 pint fresh oysters

2 large eggs, beaten lightly

Place croutons in a large bowl and set them aside. Melt the butter in a frying pan and sauté the onions and celery over medium heat for 7 minutes, or until tender. Add the liver and sauté for an additional minute, or until the liver is firm.

Pour the onions and butter over the croutons. Add the seasonings and stir well. Add the oysters and eggs and mix together. Add a little water if the mixture seems dry. Allow to cool and then stuff the turkey.

Serving Pieces

Containers in the shape of a plum pudding, turkey, or squash were suggested for candy or tea. A turkey set of Wedgewood included a platter and six plates. Cut glass in the shape of a horn of plenty, or cornucopia, was suggested to hold fruit or flowers.

Recipes adapted from the *Kansas City Star*, 1907

GUMBO À LA CREOLE

SERVES 4

2–3 pounds chicken, cut up

8 tablespoons butter

2 cups okra, sliced thick

3 medium tomatoes, chopped

1 medium onion, chopped

1 teaspoon cayenne pepper sauce

1 teaspoon fresh or dried thyme

½ teaspoon salt

2 tablespoons chopped fresh parsley

2 quarts water

Rice and crusty French bread, for serving

In a large stockpot, fry the chicken in the melted butter over medium-high heat until browned on all sides. Add the remaining ingredients, except the water, and cook over medium-low heat until everything starts to turn dark brown, but do not burn. Stir often.

Once the mixture has turned dark brown, add the water and stir completely. Cover and cook over low heat for about an hour. If the gumbo is too thick, add a little more water. Taste for seasoning and serve over rice with French bread.

Recipe adapted from the *St. Louis Republic*, 1890

HAMBURG STEAK

SERVES 4

1 pound lean ground beef

1 teaspoon salt

½ onion, chopped

1 tablespoon oil

BROWN SAUCE

2 tablespoons pan drippings or butter

2 teaspoons flour

2 cups water or broth

Salt and pepper to taste

Mix all ingredients (except the oil) well and shape into four 1-inch-thick patties. Heat the oil in a frying pan over medium-high heat.

Add the patties and cook for 4 minutes. Flip and cook for another 2 minutes for medium-rare patties. Cover with a lid for more well-done patties and cook in 2-minute increments.

To make the sauce, brown the pan drippings or butter in a saucepan. Add the flour and cook over medium heat until flour is lightly browned. Add water or broth and stir until smooth and thick. Salt and pepper to taste.

Recipe adapted from the *Sioux City* (Iowa) *Journal*, 1900

DELMONICO POTATOES

SERVES 2–4

Melted butter

3 large white or yellow potatoes, peeled and cooked

¼ cup grated cheese

Salt and pepper to taste

1¼ cups White Sauce (recipe follows)

Bread crumbs

Butter a baking dish. Cut potatoes into ½-inch cubes to make 2 cups. Put a layer of potatoes into the baking dish. Sprinkle with cheese, salt and pepper and half the sauce. Repeat. Cover the top with bread crumbs and drizzle with butter. Bake in a 375° oven for about 20 minutes or until the crumbs are brown.

Recipe adapted from *Aberdeen* (South Dakota) *Daily American*, 1910

WHITE SAUCE

MAKES 2 CUPS

4 tablespoons butter

6 tablespoons flour

½ teaspoon salt

¼ teaspoon freshly ground pepper

2 cups milk

Melt the butter in a medium saucepan over medium heat. When the butter begins to bubble, add the flour and seasonings. Stir and cook 2 to 3 minutes to allow the flour to cook. Gradually add the milk and whisk constantly until the sauce thickens.

Recipe adapted from Washington's *Morning Olympian*, 1907

BROWNED SWEET POTATOES

SERVES 4

4 large sweet potatoes

4 tablespoons butter, melted

4 tablespoons brown sugar

Peel and cut the sweet potatoes in half. Steam or boil until tender. Place the potatoes on a greased or lined baking sheet. Brush each with a tablespoon of the butter and sugar. Broil until golden.

Place Cards

Place cards establish where guests would sit. The paper suggested they could be shaped like a wishbone or a football. Traditional silver holders as well as the new 1905 novelties of miniature pigs, turkeys, and geese were suggested.

To have some fun with the cards, use the guest's initials and make up words that best describe the guest and their favorite hobby instead of using their name. For example, a female guest's initials are A. S.; she finds the words *Always Sings* and takes her seat at the card that matches her initials and description.

Recipe adapted from the *Fort Worth Telegram*, 1907

PUMPKIN PIE

MAKE ONE 9-INCH PIE

2 cups pumpkin puree

1 teaspoon ground cinnamon

¾ cup honey

½ teaspoon freshly grated nutmeg

½ teaspoon salt

3 eggs, beaten

1 cup evaporated milk

1 single 9-inch piecrust (page 119), unbaked

In a large bowl, combine all the ingredients except for the milk and piecrust.

Mix well and then stir in the milk. Continue stirring until completely blended.

Pour the mixture into the piecrust and bake at 375°F for 45 to 50 minutes. The pie is done when a knife inserted comes out clean.

Cool slightly before cutting and serving.

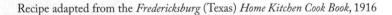

Recipe adapted from the *Fredericksburg* (Texas) *Home Kitchen Cook Book*, 1916

STRAWBERRY PIE

MAKES ONE 9-INCH PIE

1 double Piecrust (page 119)

1 quart strawberries

¼ cup sugar

Butter

Whipped cream, for serving

Line a 9-inch pie pan with one of the crusts. Wash and hull the strawberries and allow them to drain. Add the strawberries to the pie pan and sprinkle with sugar. Dot with butter and top with the second crust. Bake in a 350°F oven for 20 to 30 minutes or until the crust is golden. Top with whipped cream.

Sentiments: In 1905 the *Idaho Statesman* suggested a way to entertain guests:

Provide guests with sheets of paper and small pencils, and ask each of them to write a Thanksgiving sentiment. The hostess collects them and reads each one aloud, while the guests try to discover the author. The person who guesses the most correctly wins a prize.

Recipe adapted from Oklahoma City's *Daily Oklahoman*, 1910

OATMEAL

SERVES 2–3

1⅓ cups oatmeal

Water

2 cups milk

Sugar, honey, or maple syrup, for serving

Place the oatmeal in a bowl, cover with water, and allow it to soak overnight. The next morning, drain off any excess water.

Place the oatmeal in a medium saucepan and add the milk. Cook over medium heat for about 15 minutes or until the oatmeal is smooth and creamy. Serve with sugar, honey, or maple syrup.

Adapted from Silver City's *Idaho Avalanche*, 1880

The bells are ringing in the Christmas morn.

CHRISTMAS

———————⟡———————

ALL ACROSS THE WEST DURING THE JOLLY SEASON OF CHRISTMAS, ranchers, businessmen, miners, and most everyone else could take a break from their duties—within reason. Church and God were the focus of the holiday. Many people did not have a tree in their own home, but their church or community gathering place often did. Christmas trees in homes became more popular as the turn of the twentieth century neared. Some churches invited orphans and poor children to help decorate and to offer them presents from Santa Claus. Choirs sang and minimal presents were handed out. Afterward, pioneers enjoyed food, drink, and merry-making. Towns across the frontier celebrated Christmas with songs, church, friends, community trees, decorations, and more.

General George Armstrong Custer's wife, Elizabeth "Libby" Bacon Custer, wrote fondly of her Christmases on the plains:

> *The most remarkable Christmases of my life have been spent on the plains, in Uncle Sam's forts. Away out on the frontier, many miles from any railroad, in a lonely little fort surrounded by Indians, army officers and their wives have not long rows of elegant shops from whose great supply of holiday goods they may purchase gifts. . . . In the*

little frontier post away out on the trackless plains of our great country where scarcely a shrub—much less anything worthy of the name of a tree—can be seen as far as the eye can reach, even amid the heat of summer, the question is how to obtain a Christmas tree for the little ones if there happen to be any in the fort. In such cases I have heard of quite a respectable Christmas tree being "faked" by splitting together several walking-sticks, fastening them upright through a hole in a soap-box, and covering them with green tissue paper, obtained from the post store. . . . One universal custom was for all of us to pass as much of the day as possible in each other's society. All day long the officers were running in and out, and everybody was wishing every other body a merry Christmas. We usually had a sleigh ride and everyone sang and laughed as we sped over the country, where there were no neighbors to be disturbed by our gayety. To secure a Christmas dinner was even more important than to procure a Christmas tree. . . . With a garrison full of perfectly healthy people with a determination to be merry despite their isolated life and dreary surroundings, the holidays were something to look forward to the year round.

No matter where they were, most pioneers recognized the day. Sometimes it was a simple meal, some prayers, and singing. A preserved orange peel to scent a drawer or a piece of candy was often a cherished gift. Santa and gifts were generally reserved for Christmas

Postcards were a cheaper alternative to sending Christmas cards and were very popular (ca. 1900s). SHERRY MONAHAN

Eve, while Christmas Day was spent in church and feasting. And greetings were shared with those near and far.

Nancy Griswold of Dryden, Missouri, was fond of John Griffin, who was serving in the War between the States. On January 1, 1864, she penned a letter to him which describes how she spent Christmas:

Dear Friend John: I received your ever welcome letter on the evening of the 14th of Nov. containing your photograph. I was very glad indeed to receive it and think it much more natural than the one I had in my possession. It finds a conspicuous place in our Album, and I thank you very much for your kindness in sending it. Geo. Phillips called on us when he was east. He appears perfectly natural, no doubt you have heard of Mary's marriage. We did not see her husband and he being a stranger in these parts we know but little about him. His name is Sears, they were married and started immediately for his place of residence. . . . We certainly have much to give thanks for, much that we are capable of comprehending as blessings. And no doubt we should look by the eye of faith on all things as blessings in disguise (though by the natural eye they would not seem as such) and give thanks to the author of every good and every perfect gift. Christmas has come and gone. The eve was spent at the church where a tree was placed loaded with presents. Santa Claus made his appearance much to the delight of the children, and the merriment of all judging from the smiling faces to be seen. I will describe his appearance as you may not have been so fortunate as to have seen him. As he is often talked of but seldom beheld. He had a long white beard resembling frost, wore a pair of spectacles a tall hat placed on the back of his head, ornamented with diminutive flags of our union. A fur coat, with a string of sleigh-bells extending over one shoulder and around his waist. Some goose wings arranged in the tops of his boots, a basket of toys was on one arm and as he came in he led a white lamb, and gave it to a little boy for whom it was *intended. Nearly all of his ornaments were given to the children, scores of bright eyes watched his movements anxiously expecting something. At length the tree was unloaded for the benefit of the older ones, nearly all received some gift from the value of a letter (and many times is highly prized) to that of sets of furs, Photographic Albums, &c, &c. Among the rest my name was called and I received a ring with my name marked on it, also a set of silver tea spoons marked with my name, they proved a perfect surprise as I had no idea of receiving such a present, Ellen also received spoons. We have since learned that they were hung on the tree by mother, or presented by her. The valuation of all the articles was thought to be over $2000. The evening was bright and pleasant, and we reached home about 10 o'clock, all passed off pleasantly. We have had but little snow yet it has been so evenly distributed that the sleighing has been pretty good, and we have improved it to some extent. You ought to see our black colts John, they are almost an exact match, spirited, yet gentle. I wish you could break away from camp life for a time at least and enjoy a drive with us on some of these cold days. You expressed a wish in your last that you might be permitted to return home in early summer and 'take in Dryden in your way.' I should be most happy to see you, as our folks also would—I have sometimes read portions of your letters to father, and he has (without intending to flatter you) an exalted opinion of your nobility. I think John that there are persons who are not moved by praise, they seem to be above what is called flattery, and move with a quiet dignity regardless of idle words. "Brave boys are they" is sung much, together with many other patriotic songs, around here. Who will care for Mother now is a favorite piece, but no doubt you are aware that I was not blessed with the power of song. I can only listen and admire, sometimes for the diversion of self. I try my voice but not at all to my satisfaction therefore my talent is buried. My dear Brother was well when last he wrote it was the next day after Christmas and he had spent that memorable day with a lady friend whom society he prizes very highly.*

Elizabeth Le Breton Gunn, who was living in Sonora, California, penned this letter to her parents on December 26, 1851.

Yesterday was Christmas Day. . . . We filled the stockings on Christmas Eve. . . . The children filled theirs. They put in wafers, pens, toothbrushes, potatoes, and gingerbread, and a little medicine. . . . They received cake and candies, nuts and raisins, a few pieces of gold and a little money, and, instead of books, some letters. Their father and I each wrote them letters, and better than all and quite unexpected, they found yours, and were delighted. In my stocking were a toothbrush and a nailbrush (the latter I wanted very much) and some cakes and a letter from Lewis. . . . We had a nice roast of pork, and I made a plum pudding. Mr. Christman gave the children some very nice presents; each of the boys a pearl handled knife with three blades, Sarah a very pretty box, and Lizzie a pair of scissors, and each a paper of macaroons.

This typical Christmas postcard (ca. 1900s) reads "The bells are ringing in the Christmas morn." SHERRY MONAHAN

Christmas Controversy

While pioneers living on the frontier enjoyed traditional Christmas festivities, many in Utah did not. Christmas in Utah, especially in Salt Lake City, in 1858 was a little contentious between the Mormons and the "Gentiles," or non-Mormons. On December 20, 1858, the San Francisco *Daily Evening Bulletin* republished a story from a Utah correspondent. The storyline read, "How the Mormon Ladies Fond of Gentile Parties Are Dealt with." Because they attended Gentile holiday parties, the church felt they needed to be told of the consequences in a very public way. The story began,

> *I have referred in former letters to the opposition which has been manifested to these parties by the Mormon leaders, and I have now ascertained the plans which they have adopted to prevent the attendance of Mormon ladies. It appears that it is designed to open the Tabernacle shortly and resume public service on Sundays; but no one will be admitted into the building without a "recommend" or pass from the bishops of the church. Well, the bishops have notified all the young ladies of their wards that none of those who attend our parties will receive a "recommend," but will be debarred from the privilege of entering the Tabernacle. Again, they are to be warned three times—once privately; next, in the presence of two or three persons; finally, in public—not to attend any Gentile gatherings; and if, after these repeated warnings, they still persist, they are to be cut off from the church.*

Texas Celebrations

General Custer's wife, Libby, shared a description of her Christmas while they were stationed in Hempstead, Texas in 1866.

We had a lovely Christmas. I fared beautifully, as some of our staff had been to San Antonio, where the stores have a good many beautiful things from Mexico. Here, we had little opportunity to buy anything, but I managed to get up some trifle for each of our circle. We had a large Christmas-tree, and Autie [George] was Santa Claus, and handed down the presents, making side-splitting remarks as each person walked up to receive his gift. The tree was well lighted. I don't know how so many tapers were gotten together. . . . Tom, who is always drumming on the piano, had a Jew's-harp given him, with an explanatory line from Autie attached, to give the piano a rest. Only our own military family were here, and Armstrong gave us a nice supper, all of his own getting up. We played games, sang songs, mostly for the chorus, danced. . . . The rooms were prettily trimmed with evergreens, and over one door a great branch of mistletoe, about which the officers sang, "Fair mistletoe! Love's opportunity! What trees that grow! Give such sweet impunity?" But it is too bad that, pretty as two or three of our women are, they belong to someone else. So kissing begins and ends with every man saluting his own wife.

Mrs. George C. Wolffarth remembered when she arrived in Estacado, Texas, in 1884: "Christmas day was warm and beautiful and we had a watermelon feast on the church house lawn. Isiah Cox . . . had stored the melons in his cellar and they were in fine condition for the Christmas feast." Yet another Texas native recalled her Christmas in Parker County, Texas, despite not having a church or public meeting facility. Resident Mrs. Mary Green, who lived there during the late 1800s, recalled, "The first Christmas in their new home came and the only place where they could hold a public celebration was a Blacksmith shop, which boasted a dirt floor. There were few children to be remembered, however ginger cookies, homemade dollies and other toys were provided."

In 1867, the pioneers living south of Libby Custer in Galveston, Texas, were treated to a history lesson on the origin of Santa Claus by their local paper, *Flake's Daily Bulletin*:

"Among the happy customs of merry Christmas, there are none more pleasing than those that cluster around the mythical Cris Kringle. While most of our customs are from the English, Cris Kringle is a genuine Dutchman, he comes from Holland, and was a citizen of New York, when New York was New Amsterdam. Santa Claus and Cris Kringle are other names for Saint Nicholas, who was alike the titular Saint of Holland and of all children." They told of how he was born on December 6, 343 in Patma City, Lycia (in

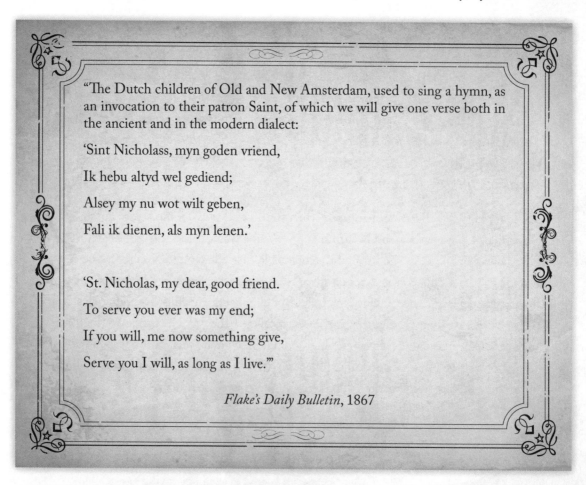

"The Dutch children of Old and New Amsterdam, used to sing a hymn, as an invocation to their patron Saint, of which we will give one verse both in the ancient and in the modern dialect:

'Sint Nicholass, myn goden vriend,

Ik hebu altyd wel gediend;

Alsey my nu wot wilt geben,

Fali ik dienen, als myn lenen.'

'St. Nicholas, my dear, good friend.

To serve you ever was my end;

If you will, me now something give,

Serve you I will, as long as I live.'"

Flake's Daily Bulletin, 1867

current-day Turkey). His parents were Catholic and as an infant instinctively fasted on Wednesdays and Fridays by refusing his mother's milk. Constantine the Great eventually made him the patron saint of sailors and children. . . . They continued, "May the traditions and customs of Saint Nicholas long resist the march of our practical civilization, which so persistently throws down all our household goods, and destroys all our pleasant folly."

A Ranch-Style Christmas Dinner

Herbert Hilsop was a newly arrived Englishman who ran the Empire Ranch in southeastern Arizona with Walter Vail. Herbert acted as the cook while they worked on securing a proper one. Being a bachelor in the remote area between Tucson and Sonoita proved challenging for Herbert when he set out to make Christmas dinner in 1876.

Herbert was very proud of his first Christmas dinner at the ranch. He penned a letter to his sister Amy in England:

> We spent Christmas as merry as we could. . . . We sat down to a festive meal, which I had taken great trouble to cook and serve up as nicely and prettily as possible, not forgetting the familiar "Wishing you a Merry Christmas" stuck in a stick at the top of the first successful plum-pudding at Empire Ranch, the inscription being in Spanish as well, so our sheepherder could see it [they had sheep on their ranch while they worked on acquiring the cattle]. . . . I surrounded the pudding with brandy and set light to it in the regular old style. Though we are in a rough country we try to enjoy ourselves sometimes, not being able to get a wild turkey, we got four wild ducks. . . . I trussed these as best I could and I thought equal to a poulterer, only I had no sage and onions but plenty of bread crumbs, salt, pepper, and butter, a beautiful dish of nice brown mashed potatoes which I

ornamented to the best of my ability, along with plum-pudding and brandy-sauce, good coffee and two bottles of whiskey—the best we could get in the country.

I could not procure all the articles necessary for the pudding, but substituted them as best I could. In the place of beef suet I had to use mutton fat and could not procure citron on or lemons, but in the place of lemon I put an orange and chopped up the peel.

In the nineteenth century, mince pie was not round like other pies but was oblong to resemble the manger in which Jesus was laid in Bethlehem. The spices used in the pie were meant to symbolize the gifts the three Wise Men brought to the baby. Anyone eating mince pie on Christmas was supposed to have a year full of good luck.

A Child's Christmas in Nebraska

In 1880 Ella Oblinger was a ten-year-old girl living with her parents in Nebraska. In January of that year, she wrote a letter to her grandparents to tell them about her Christmas.

January 12th 1880

Dear Grand Pa and Grand Ma

As Ma was writing I thought I would write you a few lines to let you know we are all well there was the sweetest little baby here last night Mr. Johnsons staid here all night

Mr. Johnson preaches here every two weeks Maggie &
Stella are in bed asleep & I must tell you how I spent
Christmas eve we all went to see a Christmas tree on
Christmas eve. I got a new red oil calico dress I will
send you a piece of them [and?] each one of us girls got a
doll and uncle Giles put a book on for sabra and me &
each one of us girls a string with candy and raisins on
it. Christmas day we all went to uncle Gileses & New-
years we were invited to a Newyears dinner up to Mr.
Bumgardners. I eat till I nearly bursted eating oysters
& good things. I will tell you what I study Reading
and Arithmatic & Spelling & Geography & Writing
Christmas night I got pair of stockings & a nice new
book called the three white kittens & Sabra & Maggie
both got a new pair of stockings & primer books &
Newyears all of us girls got a candy apple apeice & a
paper sack of mixed candy & a paper sach of raisins.
From your Grand child, Ella 'E' Oblinger.

A Merry Christmas
I wish you not the Christmas cheer,
That with time's passing fades away—
But that which lasts from year to year,
And gains new lustre with each day.

*Because postcards were so popular on the frontier, shoppers had
a wide variety to choose from. Many were religious, funny, or
sentimental (ca. 1900s).* SHERRY MONAHAN

Fruitcake

Fruitcake was often the centerpiece of feasts during
Thanksgiving, Christmas, and New Year's dinners. In
1882 the *Standard* of Clarksville, Texas, ran a story that demonstrated just how important
it was: "CHRISTMAS! . . . To-morrow comes the much-loved Christmas Day. . . . First:
the morning of necessity must open with a nogg of eggs and sugar and something to cook

it, so that it will not taste raw, then rich fruit-cake comes in course, then a Christmas turkey dressed with fresh oysters, and a little generous wine to wash it down."

Plenty of frontier housewives prided themselves on making their own fruitcake. Some were also content to simply buy theirs from their local merchant if they could. In 1892 fruitcake sold for $0.50 per pound, which today would equal $12.80 per pound, but by 1900 the price had dropped to $0.30. Merchants began advertising as early as October for their fruitcakes. There were several varieties of fruitcake, including Parisian, black, farmer's, poor man's, and a host of others using the ingredients that were on hand when they were being made.

Decorating for Christmas

If instead of writing a Christmas welcome to the thousands of women to whom this Christmas Journal will go, I could enter the homes myself and talk with you, it would please me far better than using this greeting made formal by pen and paper. Perhaps in the midst of Christmas carols and Christmas cheer there would be no opportunity to take me about your homes and show me what ingenuity, taste and thought you have given to ornamenting and making pleasant the blessed abode for your husband and children. I might not be permitted, for want of time on your part, to know the history of each gift which you have planned and thought out late at night, and in the calm of early morning. But still, I dearly wish that I might enter your comfortable homes, and hear of your aims, your blessings and perplexities, your sorrows. In wishing all the good things this world gives may descend on the households to which the Journal goes, I would that it might give me the special privilege to let me enter those thousands of little makeshifts for home throughout our land that the busy women of limited means have set up; the dingy rooms under the eaves, where deft fingers have made such transformations; the little apartments where is ever semi-twilight, where God's beautiful twilight comes in thru the narrow windows—ah, it is to you, brave, but lonely women, if any such read these words, that I wish to send my love, and whatever of courage deep felt words can convey. The widows, the girl bachelors, the solitary old maids, all of you who are so much to me, I envy the printed and pictured sheets of this holiday Journal, the cheer and comfort they carry.

Elizabeth B. Custer
Ladies Home Journal, 1890

In addition to planning Christmas meals, decorating the home was also important. Decorations varied from simple to extravagant. Christmas trees were adorned with strands of popped corn and cranberries and were often illuminated with candles. As early as the mid-1800s, newspapers contained ads for gift ideas, menus, games, and trees, wreaths, and greens. One San Francisco merchant advertised "Christmas Trees. Evergreens and

The Tacoma Daily News *published this story with tips on how to decorate a Christmas tree in their December 10, 1898, issue.* TACOMA DAILY NEWS, DECEMBER 10, 1898

Decorations of all kinds, together with Bouquets and Wreaths, can be found (at reasonable rates) at the depot of G. Bernstein."

Everyone from local merchants to newspaper correspondents offered suggestions and trends for decorating. Washington's *Tacoma Daily News* shared an in-depth piece with their suggestions. They felt that Christmas would not be nearly as cheerful without decorations. They reported, "Weeks before Christmas men are scouring the northern mountain slopes for the fir, the spruce, the pine and the balsam trees. . . . The tree is in many houses the real center of the Christmas interest. The gifts, of the entire household are placed upon it for distribution on Christmas eve."

The Grand Forks, North Dakota's *Daily Herald* offered some insight into the Christmas tree market in 1897. They reported,

> *The Young Folks Like Them and Almost Every Home Will Have One. The Christmas tree is a necessary article of commerce. It costs nothing to chop one, even if it isn't decorated much, it satisfies the youth who would undoubtedly feel quite discontented without one. The Christmas tree ranges in size from the puny two-footer to the imposing ceiling scraper. The latter are used principally by the church and schools for the holiday entertainments and of course bring higher prices. These sometimes retail for as much as $10 [$294 today] a piece. The smaller trees, however, are more commonly used and it might be added that they are more in touch with the pocketbooks of the average individual. Men who make a business of supplying trees in the large cities usually commence their labors ten days before Christmas, for the average tree will not keep much longer than that time."*

The Hotel Metropole in Bismarck, North Dakota, treated its citizens to a delectable Christmas dinner in 1898. Items included Smithfield ham, turkey, antelope, bluefish, assorted vegetables, and the traditional English plum pudding. COURTESY OF THE NEW YORK PUBLIC LIBRARY

As Christmas trees became a traditional decoration in homes across the frontier, some had them not only in their parlors or family rooms but in their dining rooms as well. The Campbells of St. Louis were well-known for the elaborate parties during the mid-1800s at their posh Lucas Place home. Robert was an Irish immigrant who joined the fur trade and became one of the wealthiest men in Missouri. He had a real estate empire, with land in Texas, Kansas, and elsewhere. He served as president of two banks and managed the Southern Hotel, which was one of the finest hotel in St. Louis. His wife Virginia was a North Carolina native and gained a well-earned reputation as a graceful hostess. The Campbells' parties were one of the most sought-after social engagements. Their Lucas Place home was decorated in lavish style, and after Robert and Virginia passed away, their

The Campbells decked their house in 1895 with elaborate Christmas decor from the Victorian era that featured Santa and his reindeer. COURTESY OF THE LIBRARY OF CONGRESS

son Hugh kept up the family tradition. In the late 1890s, the family home was decorated for Christmas with evergreens, bows, ribbons, and figurines. In addition to the rest of the home, the dining room table offered an elaborate reindeer display.

Ellinor Dale Runcie thoroughly enjoyed decorating her aunt Ellie Davidson's Christmas tree while visiting her Washington Street home in San Francisco. Ellinor was from St.

Joseph, Missouri, and had often visited her aunt and cousin Ellinor during the late 1800s. It seems her 1900 Christmas was very memorable, and she penned a letter home to her mother about it.

My darling Mother . . . But now for our Christmas. Monday morning, I ran to the grocer's, for cranberries and popcorn, which I proceeded to pop, string etc., and was busily occupied all morning, Ellinor being gone to deliver presents, and other matters. After lunch, I got all the trimmings together and began my very enjoyable task of decking the little tree, while Ellinor rested up in my room on the reclining chair, in her warm, crimson dressing gown, and strung popcorn and berries with lightning rapidity. After a while she joined me in the parlor (the middle room where the tree is) and helped festoon the bough etc. until Miss Faster arrived for the music lesson. They let me stay in the room and trim, while the reading of Beethoven progressed, and all was nearly ready by the time they had stopped. Then Miss F. had to admire the tree. Some mistletoe hung from the chandelier and Ellinor roguishly drew the little woman beneath it and gave her a hearty kiss. She arranged sheets over the tree box and over stools, to resemble a rugged mountain slope, and heaped delicious looking bundles around in rich confusion. That evening, all being ready, E. slipped out while we were all at dinner, and lighted the tree, so that when we entered, there was the bright little thing shining away for all it was worth. Mr. and Mrs Lent appeared unexpectedly from next door to thank the Dr. for a Xmas wreath, but after they left, the gifts were delivered; E. and I examining ours by the light of the Christmas tree candles. Ellinor got lots of beautiful presents. She gave me a pretty silver hat pin, an iron candle stick in the shape of a griffin, holding a red candle, and she presented me also with her picture. Aunt Ellie gave me a perfectly exquisite napkin ring with my monogram on it, and a photograph of Uncle George in his academic robes. Lil Kerr sent me a pretty collar she made, Swann, a red burnt leather card case with a big fleur de lis on one side, and my initials on the other. There was a deep note of sadness for me, in the answer from Norway to my letter to Anna

Sinding. Her husband writes that she died two years ago, at the birth of her third child. He sent me her picture, and those of the three children, including his own taken with the baby. . . . Next morning, I went to a beautiful service at Trinity Church, where I caught a glimpse of Mrs. Ashburner, who, by the way, had sent me a Christmas card. On returning, I found at my lunch plate, a great, beautiful bunch of violets sent me by Dr. Fraser, with an affectionate greeting and a P.S. to "please come and see me." Miss Lawlor also wrote me a very kind note and sent it with a card. . . . I got home just in time for the turkey and plum-pudding. Aunt Ellie looked very festive in a white satin & lace front newly made her by Ellinor. The latter had put huckleberry sprays about in effective places, and some magnificent Anna Hobart pinks were in the centre of the table. These pinks are fourteen or fifteen dollars a dozen—Dr. Frazer sent them. After dinner the tree was decked with fresh candles by Tom and me and lighted by Ellinor who takes joy in touching off each little colored taper. I sang two carols, "God Rest Ye Merry, Gentlemen," and Luther's hymn. Carols sung at the ladies' request, who doubtless thought I would feel more at home if allowed to warble. Ellinor is fascinated by the songs I gave her, and the picture of the counters is one she has long wanted. I gave Aunt Ellie a copy (small one) of Rossetti's "Dante at the Bier of Beatrice." I gave Miss M. a heart-shaped fancy box of candy, Uncle George a little tea spoon, Tom the cutest bronze mouse about this big (drawing)! The two girls I presented with a Japanese silk handkerchief apiece. I presented Tom the mouse, at Ellinor's suggestion, on a small trap containing a piece of cheese, and with this legend attached to its tail, on a long strip of paper. "I may not be full grown yet, but by gosh . . . you just set Diablo on to me!" Aunt Ellie got Tom a toy automobile, which he wanted very much! Thursday I cleaned my room; and that morning received from Mama a handsome copy of "Eleanor," with a Christmas card on which was written "With best love to my Ellinor," and a sweet Christmas message in our dear German she and I are so fond of.

I also was very much pleased to get a photograph of the school and a pretty one of the two Rhoades sisters. Shall write to thank them as soon as I can possibly find time. Ellinor and I were called away Thursday afternoon from "Eleanor" by a caller, who proved to be Mrs. Montague's niece, Miss Wright, who was very pleasant. I find the San Francisco people have good deal of ease of manner and quiet assurance. Ellinor and I took a walk late in the afternoon, to the drug store, and on returning found Aunt Ellie wanted oysters for Uncle George's supper, he being laid up all Christmas day with neuralgia. E. was tired, so I insisted on going alone for the oysters, and brought them safely to hand. Ellinor in the meantime, was yearning for a lark, and after dinner, what did we do, but go off to the "Grand" to see "An Officer of the Second" an English war drama. Ellinor had never seen a heavy villain, and she enjoyed our lark, being treated to not only the heaviest kind of villain but also to his villainess! And all for fifteen cents. . . . With much love to all, and thanks for the Christmas presents. Tell Aunt Anne I used her handkerchief Christmas day—Will write to Blessing soon—. . . . Lovingly, Ellie

Of all
The Merry
Christmas Days
You've known in old December,
May this one be the happiest,—
The best you can
remember.

Receiving a simple postcard back in the day was a big deal to pioneers who longed to hear from their loved ones (ca. 1900s). SHERRY MONAHAN

A Ranch Christmas

In contrast to a city Christmas in the West, Mrs. Clarice Richards wrote of Christmas on her ranch in Elbert County, Colorado. She and her husband Jarvis were Ohio natives who settled there in 1900. Twenty years later she penned a book called *A Tenderfoot Bride: Tales from an Old Ranch*. In it she wrote,

> *Within a radius of many miles there were only three small children, and about them our Christmas festivities revolved. They furnished the excuse for the tree, but no work was too pressing, no snow too deep to prevent the boys from bringing the Christmas tree and greens from a small clump of pines which stood on top of a distant hill, like a dark green island in the midst of the prairie sea. Early on Christmas morning Steve started out with gaily bedecked baskets for the Mexicans, and at the ranch the greatest excitement prevailed. I dashed frantically between the bunkhouse and our kitchen to be certain that nothing was forgotten. The big turkeys were stuffed to the point of bursting, all the "trimmings" were in readiness, and the last savory mince pies were in the ovens.*

She also observed,

> *The boys spent most of the morning "slicking up" and put on their red neckties, the outward and visible sign of some important event, then passed the remaining hours sitting around anxiously awaiting the arrival of the guests of honor and—dinner. Christmas was our one great annual celebration, a day of cheer and happiness, in which everyone joyously shared. It was a new experience in the life of the undomesticated cow-puncher, but he took as much satisfaction in the fact that "Our tree was a whole lot prettier than the one I've saw in town" as though he had won a roping contest.*

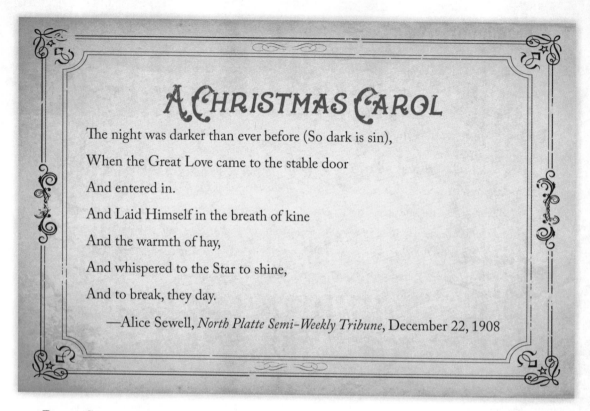

A Christmas Carol

The night was darker than ever before (So dark is sin),

When the Great Love came to the stable door

And entered in.

And Laid Himself in the breath of kine

And the warmth of hay,

And whispered to the Star to shine,

And to break, they day.

—Alice Sewell, *North Platte Semi-Weekly Tribune*, December 22, 1908

Bear Sign

Many cowboys celebrated Christmas much differently than those of the homesteading pioneers. Cowboy Andy Adams recalled his Christmas while he was working on the range in Wyoming. His Christmas treat was something cowboys called "bear sign," which meant doughnuts.

Well, three days before Christmas, just when things were looking gloomiest, there drifted up from the Cheyenne country one of the old timers. He had been working out in the

Panhandle country, New Mexico, and the devil knows where, since he had left that range. He had shown no signs of letting up at eleven o'clock the first night, when he happened to mention where he was the Christmas before. "There was a little woman at the ranch," said he, "wife of the owner, and I was helping her get up dinner, as we had quite a number of folks at the ranch. She asked me to make the bear sign—doughnuts, she called them—and I did, though she had to show me how. Well, fellows, you ought to have seen them—just sweet enough, browned to a turn, and enough to last a week."

They were so impressed with this story that they made him stay on and make bear sign for their outfit through spring. Adams wrote, "After dinner our man threw off his overshirt, unbuttoned his red undershirt and turned it in until you could see the hair on his breast. Rolling up his sleeves, he flew at his job once more. He was getting his work reduced to a science by this time. He rolled his dough, cut his dough, and turned out the fine brown bear sign to the satisfaction of all."

A couple of days later, word had spread about their bear sign man in camp. Adams continued,

The next day was Christmas, but he had no respect for a holiday, and made up a large batch of dough before breakfast. It was a good thing he did, for early that morning "Original" John Smith and four of his peelers rode in from the west, their horses all covered with frost. They must have started at daybreak—it was a good twenty-two mile ride. They wanted us to believe that they had simply come over to spend Christmas with us. Company that way, you can't say anything. But the easy manner in which they gravitated around that tub—not even waiting to be invited—told a different tale. They were not nearly satisfied by noon.

A Montana Christmas

While they weren't eating bear sign, the pioneers of Anaconda, Montana, who dined at the Montana Hotel were thoroughly satisfied. Their Christmas dinner menu was extensive and included trendy dishes of the time. The *Anaconda Standard* reported, "The traditions of the Montana hotel were well maintained yesterday and a Christmas dinner fully equal of those famous ones which have preceded I was served." Items included canapé americain, bluepoints, consommé Rothschild, cheese straws, planked whitefish, broiled lobster Montpelier, prime rib of beef demi-glace, young turkey, mashed and sweet potatoes, and frozen egg nog. It also included local items like mountain quail and Flathead Indian Reservation roast loin of buffalo

This 1900 photo shows the Flathead Indians holding a pre-Christmas family gatherings on the west side of Glacier National Park, in the dense forest of evergreen trees that skirt the Rocky Mountains. Eleven of them posed around a Christmas tree in front of a tepee. COURTESY OF THE LIBRARY OF CONGRESS

with game sauce. Many of the Flathead Indians celebrated Christmas because they had been Christianized in the nineteenth century by Father Pierre-Jean De Smet during his missionary days in the area.

Baking and Decorating

Baking and decorating were, and still are, synonymous with Christmas. Toward the latter part of the nineteenth century, the *Idaho Statesman* ran a detailed story on how to decorate the home with holly, berries, and evergreen. Avis Ellen Alden was credited with the story.

> *The pretty custom of decorating our homes with evergreens and berries at this festive season should not be allowed to die out. . . . Even when the greenery has to be bought the outlay need not be great and the trouble bestowed on the decorations is certainly well repaid. The mistletoe bough is the first thing to be considered. The first name was the "kissing bush" and we know that it retains its property of rendering anyone liable to be kissed who lingers beneath it[s] shadow, even to this day.*

> *Buy as big a branch as you can afford. Don't cut it up, but hank [hang] it just as it is in the middle of the hall. If there is a central lamp and the ceiling in sufficiently lofty the mistletoe can depend from the lamp; if this is impracticable, there will perhaps be a hook in the ceiling of a beam onto which a nail may be knocked.*

She discussed wreaths next in her article and stated those living in the country with access to abundant greenery should have thick garlands for halls and landings. She suggested smaller ones for the dining room. As for the types of green, she preferred holly, but noted it could be more expensive, especially if it contained berries. Alden recommended supplementing the greens with yew and bay. For the wreaths, she suggested laurel, but not ivy since the smell was too strong for most rooms. In addition to all the natural greens, she advised the lady of the house to purchase artificial holly berries that were prestrung to weave into the natural decor.

To further adorn the greens she wrote,

> *Paper roses, also, are not to be despised; they look very nice in wreaths which are to be hung high up, or which decorate large rooms, such as a school-room or a kitchen. These flowers are very easily made by cutting out four discs of white or pale pink paper, and scalloping them to represent the rose petals; then threading all four on a wire and pinching them up into the shape of the flower; no center need to be added, as these roses are only to be seen from a distance.*

> *Pretty devices and mottoes can be made by covering cardboard or thin wood boards with red paper and sticking letter upon it cut out in white wadding—"Welcome," "A Merry Christmas," etc.*

> *A family I know produced a very good effect in this way on their stairs, which faced the hall door; the side of each step being faced with red, and the words "A Merry Christmas to All Our Friends" in white letters, a word or two on each step all down the flight. The appearance of this welcome from the entrance was most cheery.*

The technique of frosting or flocking Christmas trees and other decorations isn't a twentieth-century tradition. In fact, Victorian pioneers were doing it all over the West. Ms. Alden provided tips on how to do this in the home: "Frosting is another thing much liked by some people, and the effect can be obtained in various ways; either by sprinkling some of the packets of 'frost powder' over leaves previously painted with thin gum, or by using ponded alum for the purpose. Frayed out wadding gives a good appearance of snow and looks pretty when gummed here and there upon a wreath of laurel."

Christmas Tree Guessing Game: Essentially, this is "I spy" for the tree, but with a rhyming twist. Players gather around the tree, and someone starts by finding a decoration on the tree, like a reindeer. That person says, "On the branches I behold some creature made of gold." The person with the correct response would say, "The object that you see is a reindeer on the tree." The rhyming questions and responses can be changed, and the game can be played until all the ornaments have been located.

Ms. Alden cautioned against decorating the drawing room, but if one thought it was necessary, she suggested the mirrors and pictures could be adorned with greens. Her last tips included the following: "The best sprig of holly must be saved for the plum pudding before it comes to table on Christmas Day. Have common scissors at hand for your decorations, as not to spoil the good ones; black thread, wire and string of different thicknesses. Should the evergreen be dirty when bought give them a good bath before using them, but take care that they are well dried after."

The *Chillicothe Constitution* in Missouri offered similar decorating ideas for the home but went into great detail about the dining room table.

> *In serving Christmas dinner the table should* appeal to the eye, *as well as to the stomach, and the hostess should look well to the setting of the festive board and the decorations. To be a model dinner, the hostess requires a perfectly appointed table, well cooked, temping food, and the correct serving of the same. . . . Christmas dinners come late*

Place Cards

Dainty cards made of heavy white or cream paper; sometimes three or four leaves are fastened together with a little bow of ribbon. A spray of holly, mistletoe, bittersweet berries, or a little snow scene is done in watercolors on the cover is especially suitable for the Christmastide. Below are given a variety of quotations appropriate for these dainty holiday souvenirs.

"Christmas is coming, and what will it bring?

Many a pleasant and gladdening thing;

Meetings and greetings, and innocent mirth:

All that is brightest and best on the earth."

"Sure Christmas is a happy time,

In spite of wintry weather,

For laugh and song, and jest go 'round

When dear friends meet together;

And hearts are warm, and eyes beam bright

In the ruddy glow of Christmas night."

"Again at Christmas did we weave

The holly round the Christmas hearth,

The silent snow possessed the earth;

And calmly fell on Christmas eve."

"As Christmas offerings meet your eyes,

Still closer be sweet friendship's ties."

"Joy and plenty in the cottage,

Peace and feasting in the hall;

And the voices of the children,

Sing out clear above it all; - A merry Christmas."

"May health and joy, and peace be thine
Upon this Christmas day,
And happy faces round thee shine
As plenteous as the flowers in May."

"Christmas comes, let every heart
In Christmas customs bear its part:
The 'old' be 'young' the sad be gay,
And smiles chase every care away."

"Again the festive season's here,
With all that can delight and cheer;
O, may you nothing lack each day,
But find fresh blessings strewn your way."

"Now Christmas comes with hearty cheer.
May kindly thoughts go 'round,
And bring to you a glad New Year,
With peace and plenty crowned."

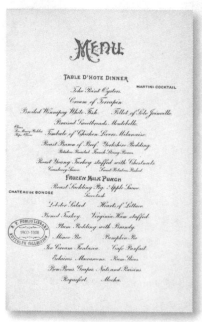

Portland, Oregon's residents were treated to a delicious Christmas dinner in 1907. The Portland Hotel offered oysters, roast beef, whitefish, turkey, sweet potatoes, plum pudding, pumpkin pie, éclairs, macaroons, and bonbons.

on Christmas day, whether it be a noon-day dinner served at three o'clock or a dinner served at six. In either case, the light falls before the dinner is over, and there must be artificial light.

It is a pretty plan to set the table with candles and to light them in the middle of dinner. A good time for this is when the turkey is taken off and the dessert is brought in. It is a time-honored custom to place the turkey on the table before the guests come in or to set forth the ducks, geese, the roast of beef, or loin of pork—whatever may be the Christmas bird. But in these later and more pampered days [1905] the stomach rebels against the

sudden plunge into the roast, and the palate demands a relish—oysters, soup, fish, and
goodness know what all! The roast comes later, flanked with green salad and vegetables
with the mound of cranberries. . . . Every Christmas dinner must have its touch of
holly, every dinner its bit of green, every Christmas dinner its Christmas motto in one
form or another and every Christmas dinner must have its own peculiar menu.

Table Decorations

Cover the table with a red tablecloth. Suspend a Santa Claus at the top of the chandelier and tie four red ribbons long enough to reach each corner of the table to him. Tie small children's Christmas toys to the ribbons' ends to mimic Santa dropping gifts down the chimney.

Cut place cards into the shapes of Santa's reindeer.

Use a snowy white tablecloth decorated with holly leaves and make a centerpiece of glossy holly leaves. Add silver candlesticks and silver bonbon dishes.

Make a flat wreath of holly tied with bows that have red berries on them. Place this around the base of a silver candelabra or candleholders.

Provide each guest with a tiny silk stocking filled with bonbons.

Wrap gifts in colorful tissue paper and adorn each with a Christmas message, some holly, or mistletoe.

Christmas Gifts

The list of gift suggestions that were advertised in local papers ran the gamut from fun to practical and included items for adults and children alike. Here's just a small sampling of nineteenth-century Christmas presents:

Books

Writing desks and portfolios

Tourists' cases and diaries

Chess- and backgammon boards

Fancy stationery

Photographic albums

Gold pens

Choice teas

Sewing machines

Stoves

Fancy French or American bonbons

Glove boxes

Musical instruments

Knives

Clothing and material

Hats

China, tea sets, cut glass, and dinnerware

Kid, bisque, and china dolls and doll furniture,

Mechanical trains, animals, and wooden toys

Drums, harmonicas, and trumpets

Fire trucks, hook and ladders, and hose carts

Hobby horses

Blocks

Games

Lamps

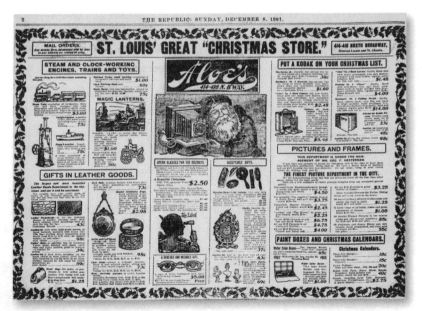

St. Louis residents viewed ads like these to shop for Christmas gifts. Trains, leather goods, cameras, opera glasses, picture frames, and desk items were some of their many choices. This one appeared in the St. Louis Republic *on December 8, 1901.* ST. LOUIS REPUBLIC, DECEMBER 8, 1901

Money could also be given as a gift, but according to the *Red Cloud Chief* in Nebraska, you had to give it in a certain way: "'If, after thinking for a long time, you cannot decide what she (my poor girl friend) would like best,' writes Ruth Ashmore, in advising girls as to their Christmas-giving; 'and you know her well enough to leave to her the choice of the gift, and less like that which is so hardly earned by her; trouble yourself to go to the bank and put it in gold, or at least in a new bank note, and enclose it in a tiny little purse.'"

Christmas Foods

The *El Paso Herald* printed a full day's menu for Christmas, which included items from breakfast through supper. For breakfast, they suggested oranges, cereal, cream, ham, eggs on toast, hot rolls, pancakes, and coffee. For the afternoon meal, celery consommé, roast turkey, chicken, rice croquettes, sweet potatoes, baked onions, parsnips, egg salad, pickles, salted almonds, mince pie, plum pudding, nuts, candies, raisins, orange ice, and coffee. The evening meal included olives, cold turkey, escalloped oysters, cold slaw (as it was spelled back in the day), raisin brown bread, cranberry jelly, pineapple ice, assorted cakes, and coffee. Funny enough, right below this menu an ad by Nations store was placed that read, "O'possums that make your mouth water."

In 1885, Ethel Hertslet, an English immigrant, wrote home about her Christmas in Lake County, California, "Now, you really must hear about my Christmas dinner!" Even though she was reared in a home with a nanny and cook, she was taught the basics of cooking before she left for America, and her cooking and traditions for her holiday meal reflected the fact that she was a native of England. She was proud that she was able to cook her family's first Christmas dinner by herself: "The plum-pudding and mince-pies were all that could be desired, and we had also tipsy cake, Victoria sandwiches, meringues, and dessert."

White Table Decorations

Set a small Christmas tree on the table, place wisps of cotton along the branches, and sprinkle it with diamond dust. Place a glass prism to imitate an icicle and add strings of popcorn and silver cord. Place a silver star atop the tree. Wrap your guest's gifts in all white paper and tie with a white ribbon to produce a "snowy" effect.

Red Table Decorations

Trim the sideboard tree with scarlet-red ribbons, holly, and red poinsettias. Hang white bells with red ribbons from the chandelier. Holly can be used to decorate paper napkins and doilies. Small Santa Clause figures can be placed around the table.

Christmas Carols

Christmas caroling and singing songs were very popular pastimes and were enjoyed in churches, schools, at home, and at people's doors. These are some favorite songs:

"It Came Upon a Midnight Clear"

"Jolly Old St. Nicholas"

"First Christmas Gifts"

"A Christmas Tree"

"Christmas Joys"

"Every Boy and Girl"

"Christmas Bells"

"Little Town of Bethlehem"

"Only One Reindeer"

"Kris Kringle"

"Night After Christmas"

Victorian Christmas Tree Decorations

White or colored popcorn garland

Cranberry garland

Popcorn balls

Candy hearts

Figures of St. Nicholas

Crosses and green leaves painted with holly berries

St. Nicholas tree topper

Cotton attached to the limbs to imitate snow

Boots and colored candies made of paper or yarn

Tinsel

White tissue paper to imitate snow

Gilt bonbons

Sprays of red-berried holly

Gilt stars (made of cardboard and covered with gold or silver paper or foil)

Candles to light the tree

Moss to place under the tree

Presents tied to the tree

Wrapped gift boxes filled with candy for your guests

Greeting Cards

Greeting cards were an eastern tradition that could easily be upheld anywhere for any occasion. Many were purchased, but others were handmade and kept as a cherished memento. They were a thoughtful, artistic remembrance for both the sender and recipient and were an extra-special way of telling someone they were fondly thought of on a holiday. Christmas cards were extremely popular, and the *Kansas City Star* reported just that:

> *For the large body of people who desire to send to their friends some slight token of continued remembrance and regard at the Christmastide the Christmas cards have become an institution. They have the great advantage that while low in price they are not cheap in estimation. They may be sent to any one, no matter how rich or how poor. They are not out of place in a palace or in a cottage. Full of the sentiment of the season, imaginative in design and artistic in execution, they are such things as one may without hesitation offer to any friend. Everyone likes to receive them. The bachelor who disdains the intricately embroidered slippers and finds more comfort in his old briarwood than in the elaborate meerschaum which he hardly dares to smoke for fear of burning it, sticks his Christmas card in the mirror or arranges it with the photographs on the mantel, and is really thankful to the sender. And the maiden who has more leather and plush abominations and small bric-a-brac*

Today postcards are rarely used except while on vacation. In the nineteenth century, they were a cheap and easy way to tell someone you were thinking of them (ca. 1900s). SHERRY MONAHAN

THE MYSTIC'S CHRISTMAS

A poem by John Greenleaf Whittier

"All hail!" the bells of Christmas rang,
"All hail!" the monks at Christmas sang,
The merry monks who kept with cheer
The gladdest day of all their year.

But still apart, unmoved thereat,
A pious elder brother sat
Silent, in his accustomed place,
With God's sweet peace upon his face.

"Why sitt'st thou thus?" his brethren cried.
"It is the blessed Christmas-tide;
The Christmas lights are all aglow,
The sacred lilies bud and blow.

"Above our heads the joy-bells ring,
Without the happy children sing,
And all God's creatures hail the morn
On which the holy Christ was born!

"Rejoice with us; no more rebuke
Our gladness with thy quiet look."
The gray monk answered: "Keep, I pray,
Even as ye list, the Lord's birthday.

"Let heathen Yule fires flicker red
Where thronged refectory feasts are spread;
With mystery-play and masque and mime
And wait-songs speed the holy time!

"The blindest faith may haply save;
The Lord accepts the things we have;
And reverence, howsoe'er it strays,
May find at last the shining ways.

"They needs must grope who cannot see,
The blade before the ear must be;
As ye are feeling I have felt,
And where ye dwell I too have dwelt.

"But now, beyond the things of sense,
Beyond occasions and events,
I know, through God's exceeding grace,
Release from form and time and place.

"I listen, from no mortal tongue,
To hear the song the angels sung;
And wait within myself to know
The Christmas lilies bud and blow.

"The outward symbols disappear
From him whose inward sight is clear;
And small must be the choice of clays
To him who fills them all with praise!

"Keep while you need it, brothers mine,
With honest zeal your Christmas sign,
But judge not him who every morn
Feels in his heart the Lord Christ born!

than she knows who to dispose of, still can always find a place for the graceful draw-ing and harmonious colors of the last Christmas card, such as PRAND, or WARD, or TUCK publish, but not those fearful satin affairs, a cross between a pin cushion and a coffin trimming, which have thrust themselves forward during the last year or two.

And again we do not recognize as true Christmas cards the flower pieces and other designs, suitable for midsummer, but having no more to do with the season or the sen-timent of the 25th of December than they have with the anniversary of the landing of the Mayflower. A Christmas card, as we understand it, is a little picture dealing with

Independence, Iowa's "Municipal Christmas" is shown in 1913. Note the lighted tree in the center of the street.
COURTESY OF THE LIBRARY OF CONGRESS

the circumstances or the ideas of Christmas. . . . We have looked over most of them which are now current, and we have failed to find one deserving of condemnation. Sweet little children dreaming of Santa Claus, fantastic dances of rabbits beneath the winter sky, royal displays or good cheer, bright visions of angels, these make up a somewhat motley crowd of subjects. But all of us know just how and where each connects with the Christmas teaching and that life of man which has so many sides, jocose and serious, prosaic and poetic, the Christmas dinner and the Christmas worship.

A Test of Memory: In 1899 the *El Paso Herald* suggested this as a "jolly game" for the holidays. It was played year-round, but at Christmas and New Year's, holiday items could be used to make it more festive. To begin, the hostess arranges assorted objects on a tray or small table in another room. Items can include anything: glasses, ornaments, toys, cups, Christmas decor, silver, and so on. She brings the tray into the room and asks her guests to memorize what is on the tray in an allotted time (say one minute). She then leaves the room with the tray and removes one item. She returns to the room with the tray and asks the guests to determine which item was removed. The first person with the correct guess wins a prize.

Christmas Recipes

These recipes and food are suggested by the Victorian pioneers themselves. The main dish for Christmas really depended upon where the pioneers lived. Some had roast turkey and goose, while others had roast pork, ribs of beef, ham, duck, or chicken. Other items include snowy white dishes like cold slaw and coconut cake.

HOT ROLLS

SERVES 6-8

1 tablespoon dry yeast

1½ cups warm water (110°F)

2 teaspoons salt

4½–5 cups bread flour

Cornmeal, for sprinkling

2 tablespoons butter, melted

In a large bowl, dissolve the yeast in ½ cup of the warm water. In a separate bowl, combine the salt and the remaining warm water. Pour this into the yeast mixture. Add 4 cups of the flour and mix well. If the dough seems sticky, gradually add additional flour as needed. Turn the dough out onto a floured surface and knead for 10 minutes, or until the dough is springy and smooth. Place the dough in a lightly oiled bowl, cover, and allow to rise in a warm place (75°F to 80°F) until doubled, about 2 hours. Punch the dough down and allow it to rise for another hour. Punch the dough down again and tear off pieces the size of a medium onion. Cup your hands and roll the dough pieces into balls. Place the dough balls 2 inches apart on a cookie sheet that has been sprinkled with cornmeal. Continuing doing this until all the dough has been used. Using the palm of your hand, flatten each roll. Cover and allow to rise until doubled, about 45 minutes. Brush the rolls with the melted butter and bake at 425°F for 15 minutes.

Recipe adapted from the *Kansas Home Cook Book*, 1874

BAKED ONIONS

SERVES 4–6

4–6 medium-size onions

Butter, for greasing the dish

¼ teaspoon salt per onion

¼ teaspoon pepper per onion

¼ cup White Sauce (page 157) per onion

¼ cup bread crumbs per onion

Peel the onions and slice ½ inch off the top and trim the bottom flat to make it stand up. Place the onions in a large pot and add enough water to come half way up the onions. Bring to a boil and cook for 10 minutes. Drain.

Grease a deep baking dish with butter and place the onions on their flat bottoms. Sprinkle with salt and pepper. Next spoon the white sauce over them and top with the bread crumbs. Bake uncovered in a 350° oven for about 20 minutes, or until golden on top.

Recipe adapted from the *Commoner*, Lincoln, Nebraska, 1905

COLD SLAW

SERVES 6-8

1 head cabbage

2 tablespoons half-and-half

2 tablespoons sugar

4 tablespoons vinegar

½ teaspoon salt

Cut the cabbage in half and remove the core from both halves. Shred the cabbage very finely and place it into a large mixing bowl. In a separate bowl make the dressing by combining the remaining ingredients. Stir to blend and pour over the cabbage.

Allow to chill for a couple of hours before serving.

Recipe adapted from Wichita, Kansas's *Thursday Afternoon Cooking Club's Cook Book*, 1922

Table Setting

For an informal family dinner, the place setting includes a dinner plate, a large folded napkin, a water tumbler, two knives (one for butter), two forks (one smaller than the other), and two teaspoons. Place a card at each place setting, and a tiny basket of flowers, a rose, or some other gift for each guest. A Christmas tree centered on the table with gifts attached for each guest can be used as well. Tiny stockings can be filled with small gifts, or miniature Christmas trees or branches of holly can also be used for decorations. Another idea is to string ribbons from above the table, either from the chandelier or the ceiling, to each guest's plate with a gift tied to the end.

When it comes to a more formal event, according to the *San Francisco Chronicle* in 1905, the base for all the course plates should be a service plate or, as it is called today, a charger. They recommended the service plate be the most expensive one used throughout the service. A bread and butter plate with a butter knife should be placed to the left of the main plate, along with a small, gilt Bohemian glass salted almond dish. Cut-glass salt and pepper shakers for each guest are set to the left of the plate, but they needed to be short and squat. Next to that are four crystal drinking goblets: for water, claret, Rhine, and Champagne.

In the main area of the table, there should be two covered vegetable dishes and one uncovered, and a glass olive "comport" or a stemmed bowl. The centerpiece should be a cut-glass flower basket filled with fresh flowers. Arrange six fairy (or tea) lights or dome-covered glass cups around the flower basket. Set four tall candlesticks with silk shades around the table. Place the turkey carving silverware next to the space where the turkey will grace the table. Olive comports, goblets, candlesticks, and flower baskets should be tall and artistic. The end of the story stated, "Your table is now ready for the turkey."

PORK ROAST

SERVES 4-6

3–4 pounds boneless pork roast

½ teaspoon salt

¼ teaspoon freshly ground pepper

¼ cup flour

Sprinkle the roast with the salt and pepper. Roll it around in the flour. Place the pork in a roasting pan, fat side up.

Bake uncovered for 2 to 2½ hours at 325°F. A meat thermometer should register 170°F when the roast is done.

Allow to stand for 15 minutes before slicing.

Recipe adapted from *Scammell's Cyclopedia of Valuable Receipts*, 1897

RIBS OF BEEF

SERVES 6–8

2- or 3-rib prime rib of beef

Flour

Cracked pepper

Salt

Dust the rib roast with flour and sprinkle all over with pepper and salt. Place the beef in a shallow roasting pans on the bone side, which creates a natural rack.

Place uncovered in a 450°F oven for 15 minutes and then reduce the heat to 350°F.

Baste the roast with pan drippings every 30 minutes.

Roast until an internal thermometer reaches desired doneness: 120°F for rare, 130°F for medium rare, 140°F for medium. Remove from the oven and allow to rest for 20 minutes before slicing. Internal temperatures can rise about 10°F after it comes out of the oven.

Recipe adapted from Virginia Campbell, mid-1800s, courtesy of the Campbell House

GINGER COOKIES

MAKES 3-4 DOZEN

1 cup molasses

½ cup sugar

1 teaspoon ginger

½ cup butter

4–4½ cups sifted all-purpose flour

1 teaspoon baking soda

¾ teaspoon salt

Combine the molasses, sugar, ginger, and butter in a saucepan and bring just to the boil. Remove from the heat and cool slightly. Put the flour, baking soda, and salt in a large mixing bowl. Stir until well blended. Add the molasses mixture to the flour and mix until blended smoothly.

Chill the dough, and then roll it out on a lightly floured board. Cut the dough into rounds and place them on a parchment-lined or greased baking sheet. Be sure to leave about an inch between the cookies, because they will spread. (You can also roll the dough into a log before chilling and then use a sharp knife to slice the cookies ⅛ to ¼ inch thick.) Bake at 375°F for 8 to 10 minutes, depending upon the size and thickness of the cookies. Remove from the cookie sheet while still slightly warm and let cool on a rack.

Recipe adapted from the *Kansas City Star*, 1903

COCONUT CAKE

MAKES 1 DOUBLE-LAYER CAKE

1 cup butter

2 cups sugar

4 eggs

1 teaspoon vanilla or lemon extract

3 cups flour

2 teaspoon baking powder

¼ teaspoon salt

1 cup milk

1–2 cups shredded coconut

Cream butter and sugar together in a large bowl.

Add the eggs and vanilla, and beat until smooth and foamy.

Combine the flour, baking powder, and salt in a small bowl, and stir.

Alternately add the flour mixture and the milk to the egg mixture, beginning and ending with the flour. Once combined, beat for about 3 minutes until light and fluffy. Pour into two greased and floured 9-inch cake pans.

Bake at 350°F for 30 to 35 minutes, or until done. Test with a toothpick.

Cool the cakes in pans for 10 minutes and then remove them to cake racks until complete cooled. Spread with your favorite frosting and coconut to your liking.

Coconut cake was a popular dessert for Christmas because of its snowy appearance and its exotic flavor.
SHERRY MONAHAN

Recipe adapted from *The Kansas Home Cook Book*, 1874

ENGLISH PLUM PUDDING

MAKES 2 LARGE PUDDINGS

Loaf of stale bread

4 cups milk

3 eggs, beaten

¾ cup butter, melted

½ cup sugar

½ cup molasses

1 teaspoon salt

¾ pound raisins, prunes, or a combination

½ teaspoon each ground cinnamon, cloves, and mace

¼ teaspoon ground nutmeg

1 teaspoon chopped orange peel

Boiling water

1 cup fruit juice

Remove the crusts from the bread, cut or shred the bread into small pieces, and measure out 4 cups. Spread them on a baking sheet. Bake at 300°F until dry, about 10 minutes, depending upon how dry the bread was to start.

Place the bread in a large bowl and cover it with the milk. Let stand for about an hour or until the milk is absorbed and the bread is soft.

Beat the bread and milk until combined and then add the eggs, butter, sugar, molasses, salt, raisins, spices, and orange peel.

Grease two 2-pound coffee cans or two 2-quart ovenproof deep dishes.

Fill each greased pan half full of batter. Cover with lids or heavy-duty aluminum foil.

Place the pudding containers in a large pot or roaster.

Pour boiling water one-third up the side of the cans and bake at 300°F for 2 hours. Test with a knife; the pudding is done it comes out clean when put into center of a pudding.

Pour juice over the puddings and allow to cool.

Refrigerate until ready to eat.

When ready to eat, heat the pudding in a water bath such as the one used for baking it, and pour more juice over it. The juice, however, will not flame as traditional spirits would.

PLUM PUDDING

Plum pudding doesn't contain plums at all. Prunes (dried plums) were originally used by Queen Elizabeth I, but since they were so costly, most people used raisins. Feel free to substitute some prunes for raisins or use a combination of the two. Beef or mutton suet (fat) was first used as a preserver so the pudding could be kept for months and be ready for Christmas.

Recipe adapted from the *Kansas Home Cook Book*, 1874

VICTORIA SANDWICHES

SERVES 4-6

Butter, equal to the weight of the eggs

Granulated sugar, equal to the weight of the eggs

4 eggs, weigh them in their shells

Flour, equal to the weight of the eggs

¼ teaspoon salt

Jam or marmalade of any kind

Cream the butter for about 5 minutes, then add the sugar and beat for about 2 to 3 minutes. Add the eggs and beat for 3 minutes. Add the flour and salt and beat for an additional five minutes. Butter a 9 x 9-inch baking pan and pour in the batter.

Bake at 350 for 20 to 25 minutes. Use a toothpick to test for doneness.

Allow the cake to cool on a wire rack. Cut the cake in half and spread the jam over the top of the bottom half of the cake. Place the other half of the cake on top and gently press the pieces together. Cut them into long finger-size pieces. Pile them like crossbars on a glass dish and serve.

These tasty treats were a traditional English Christmas dessert that pioneer immigrants made while living in the West. SHERRY MONAHAN

Recipe adapted from *Mrs. Beeton's Cookery and Household Management*, by Isabella Beeton, London, 1874

FRUITCAKE

MAKES 1 CAKE

1 cup butter

1 cup brown sugar

4 eggs, beaten

1 cup molasses

3 cups flour

1 teaspoon cinnamon

Pinch of salt

1½ teaspoons cream of tartar (see Note)

1 teaspoon baking soda (see Note)

½ teaspoon nutmeg, grated

1 cup milk

2 teaspoons brandy

2 pounds raisins

Rum flavoring (optional)

Note: You can substitute 2 teaspoons baking powder for the cream of tartar and baking soda.

In a large bowl, cream the butter and sugar together. Add the eggs, one at a time, and then the molasses and mix until blended. In a separate bowl, combine the dry ingredients and stir.

Combine milk and brandy. Alternately add the flour and milk mixture, beginning and ending with the flour, stirring after each addition. Beat for an additional 2 minutes. Gently fold in raisins.

Pour into a greased and floured loaf or ring pan and bake at 350°F for about 1 hour and 20 minutes. Check for doneness with a toothpick. Liberally apply rum flavoring, if desired.

Recipe adapted from the *San Francisco Bulletin*, 1879

BIBLIOGRAPHY

Aberdeen Daily News (SD), 7-6-1888, 11-27-1894, 12-30-1910.

Adams, Andy. *The Log of a Cowboy*. Cambridge, MA: Mifflin & Co., 1903.

Albany Democrat (OR), 6-21-1901.

Alta California (San Francisco), 8-15-1850.

Anaconda Standard, 12-26-1900.

Arizona Republic, 12-27-1905.

Bakersfield (CA), 12-24-1909.

Bellingham Herald (WA), 1-16-1910.

Bronson Pilot (KS), 12-19-1895.

California Farmer, 10-10-1867.

Cherokee Nation, cherokee.org/AboutTheNation/History/Facts/CherokeesandThanks
    giving.aspx.

Chillicothe Morning Constitution (MO), 12-16-1905.

Courier (Lincoln, NE), 11-22-1890.

Custer, Elizabeth Bacon. *Tenting on the Plains: Or General Custer in Kansas and Texas.*
    New York: Charles L. Webster & Company, 1887.

Daily Alaska Dispatch (Juneau), 7-3-1902, 6-30-1904.

Daily Boomerang (Laramie, WY), 4-4-1890.

Daily Deadwood Pioneer (Deadwood, SD), 7-6-1888.

Daily Evening Bulletin (San Francisco), 1-4-1859, 7-5-1860, 2-15-1865.

Daily Herald (Grand Forks, ND), 12-10-1894, 12-19-1897, 11-25-1900, 2-16-1908.

Daily Missourian, 5-12-1851.

Daily News (Denver, CO), 3-13-1908.

Daily Times Enterprise (Jonesboro, AR), 9-15-1904.

Daily Tribune (Bismarck, ND), 2-14-1890.

Daily Oklahoman, 10-27-1909, 6-5-1910.

Daily Oregonian, 2-14-1862, 2-3-1869.

Dakota Republican (Vermillion, SD), 11-20-1869.

Dallas Morning Herald (TX), 2-10-1866.

Dallas Morning News (TX), 2-23-1891, 1-28-1894, 2-14-1897, 11-26-1905.

Denver Daily News (CO), 12-30-1883, 1-2-1898.

Denver (Evening) Post (CO), 11-28-1895, 1-5-1901, 7-4-1904.

Duluth News Tribune (MN), 2-11-1906.

El Paso Herald (TX), 1-6-1899, 12-23-1903.

Evening Star, The (Independence, KS), 11-25-1909.

Evening Tribune (San Diego, CA), 11-13-1900.

Flake's Daily Bulletin (Galveston, TX), 12-22-1867.

Fort Smith Weekly (AR), 7-7-1869.

Fort Worth (Star) Telegram (TX), 2-2-1904, 11-12-1905, 11-21-1907.

Greene Recorder (IA), 11-26-1902.

Gordon Cumming, C. F. *Granite Crags*. London: W. Blackwood and Sons, 1884. Pdf. Retrieved from the Library of Congress, https://www.loc.gov/item/rc01000849/. (Accessed March 19, 2017.)

Helena Daily Herald (MT), 12-24-1889.

Idaho Avalanche, 5-19-1880.

Idaho (Daily) Statesman, 12-17-1899, 11-26-1905, 2-18-1906.

Idaho Register, 12-29-1899.

Independence Daily Star (KS), 11-24-1909.

Independent Record (Helena, MT), 3-21-1891.

Iola Register (KS), 8-5-1902.

Jonesboro Daily Times (AR), 2-14-1907.

Kansas City Star (MO), 12-23-1865, 11-21-1887, 12-19-1888, 2-12-1895, 11-25-1896, 7-2-1903, 8-14-1903, 2-9-1906, 11-24-1907.

Kansas City Times (MO), 8-27-1894, 2-12-1895.

Kansas Memory Collection, Kansas Historical Society, www.kshs.org.

Leavenworth Herald (KS), 6-30-1894.

Library of Congress, American Life Histories: Manuscripts from the Federal Writers' Project, 1936 to 1940. loc.gov/collections/federal-writers-project. (Accessed April 7, 2017.)

Millbrook, Minnie Dubbs. *The Diary of Rebecca Richmond.* Topeka: Kansas Historical Society, 1972.

Morning Oregonian, 11-22-1897, 11-23-1910.

Newton Daily Republican (KS), 12-1-1893.

Puget Sound Weekly Argus (Port Townsend, WA), 12-7-1871.

Record Union (Sacramento, CA), 9-14-1890.

Red Cloud Chief (NE), 12-24-1897.

Republican, The (Springfield, MA), December 23, 1894.

Richards, Clarice E. *A Tenderfoot Bride: Tales from an Old Ranch.* New York: Doubleday, Page & Company, 1920.

Riverside Enterprise (CA), 2-11-1905.

Sacramento Daily Union (CA), 1-16-1875.

Sacramento Transcript (CA), 6-4-1851.

Salt Lake Evening Telegram (UT), 12-25-1909.

Salt Lake Herald (UT*)*, 11-19-1905.

Salt Lake Telegram (UT), 11-28-1905.

San Diego Union, The (CA), 11-25-1892.

San Francisco Chronicle, 12-11-1869, 1-26-1870, 2-13-1875, 12-28-1881, 11-25-1892, 7-10-1898, 11-12-1905, 12-10-1905.

Seattle Daily Times (WA), 11-23-1901.

Seattle Sunday (WA), 7-1-1899, 2-7-1904.

Sedan Lance (KS), 11-27-1903.

St. Louis Republic (MO), 11-30-1888, 6-23-1889, 7-6-1890, 12-15-1894, 12-22-1900, 12-8-1901.

Standard (Clarksville, TX), 11-24-1882.

State Gazette (Austin, TX), 7-6-1869.

Sunday Oregonian, 12-30-1900, 7-6-1902.

Sunday World Herald (Loomis, IA), 6-28-1891.

Tacoma Daily News (WA), 1-1-1894, 12-31-1894, 12-10-1898, 3-10-1906.

Topeka Daily Capital (KS), 1-2-1901.

Ukiah Daily Journal (CA), 1-3-1908.

Valentine Democrat (NE), 12-31-1903.

Weekly Capital (Topeka, KS), 11-27-1890.

Wichita Searchlight (KS), 11-11-1905, 7-11-1908.

World Herald (Omaha, NE), 11-26-1889, 1-4-1897.

CONNECTIONS TO THE PAST

Antique Rose Emporium in Independence, Texas, sells roses that date back to the eighteenth century. antiqueroseemporium.com

The Campbell House in St. Louis offers guided tours that let you step back in time and experience an elegant home where extravagant holiday parties were thrown. campbell housemuseum.org

Empire Ranch, Sonoita, Arizona, is a visit to a nineteenth-century ranch. empireranch foundation.org/empire-ranch/history

Hotel Colorado has been open since 1893. hotelcolorado.com

Hotel del Coronodo has been open since 1888. hoteldel.com

Paas Easter Eggs—color like the pioneers did! paaseastereggs.com/history

Palace Hotel has been open since 1875. sfpalace.com

Sweet Candy Company has been making candy on the frontier since 1892. sweetcandy .com

INDEX

ABOUT THE AUTHOR

Sherry Monahan is the past president of Western Writers of America (2014–2016) and holds memberships in the James Beard Foundation, the Author's Guild, National Women's History Museum, and the Wild West History Association. Sherry is also a member of the National Genealogical Society and the Association of Professional Genealogists. She has her own column ("Frontier Fare") in *True West* magazine, where she is also a contributing editor. Her other books include *The Golden Elixir of the West, The Cowboy's Cookbook, Mrs. Earp,* and *Frontier*

Fare. Sherry's *The Cowboy's Cookbook* won a Gold Will Rogers Medallion Award in 2016. She's also written for *Cowboys and Indians* magazine and has appeared on TV in various documentaries.

Sherry is one of the original members of the Most Intrepid Western Author Posse and was sworn in as honorary Dodge City marshal during one of their "rides."